POEMS RETRIEVED

POEMS RETRIEVED
Frank O'Hara

Edited by Donald Allen
with an Introduction by Bill Berkson

City Lights / Grey Fox
San Francisco

Library of Congress Cataloging-in-Publication Data

O'Hara, Frank, 1926–1966.
[Poems. Selections]
Poems retrieved / Frank O'Hara ; edited by Donald Allen ; with an introduction by Bill Berkson.
    pages ; cm.
ISBN 978-0-87286-597-6
I. Allen, Donald, 1912–2004. II. Title.

PS3529.H28A6 2013
811'.54—dc23

2013003673

City Lights Books are published at the City Lights Bookstore
261 Columbus Avenue, San Francisco, CA 94133
www.citylights.com

For Edwin Denby
who asked, "And when
will we have the complete
poems of Frank O'Hara?"

CONTENTS

Editor's Note

Frank O'Hara was never very sanguine about publishing his poems. As early as the late spring of 1951, when his M.A. thesis, "A Byzantine Place —50 Poems and a Noh Play," won a major Hopwood award at the University of Michigan, he began to have doubts. On June 6, 1951, he wrote Jane Freilicher: "No publication goes with the Hopwood award, alas, and both Alfred Knopf and Herbert Weinstock of the same 'firm' told me it was next to impossible to publish poetry in our time. I think of this with absolute delight when I think how embarrassing my letters will be for my relatives when they have to dig my poems out of them if I ever do get published. Anyway you could fit the people I write for into your john, all at the same time without raising an eyebrow." (An irony of history: it was that "firm," Alfred A. Knopf, Inc., that published O'Hara's *Collected Poems* in 1971.)

As though to make certain his prediction would come true he proceeded throughout his short life to send poems to friends, to composers, to editors, often without bothering to retain a copy. (This, of course, was before the Xerox machine.) Many poems survive only because they were included in the Hopwood award thesis, for instance, or were carefully preserved by devoted friends and by curators of manuscript collections.

One puzzle was the "Poem" beginning "Here we are again together," which O'Hara wrote in April 1954. When Ben Weber the next year wanted poems to set as songs, O'Hara gave him his only copy of several poems including this one. Weber composed music for the first stanza and published it as his Song Opus 44, in *Folder*, No. 4, 1956. (His setting of the second stanza was not completed.) And it is only through the late Ben Weber's great kindness and generosity that I am now able to present the whole poem in this volume.

When I set out to edit the *Collected Poems* in the late sixties I felt I had little or no indication of what O'Hara himself might have included in such a volume had he lived—apart, that is, from the poems he had already published in books and magazines. True, I had studied a manuscript of some

100 early, short poems in 1961 when he wanted my advice on what to include in *Lunch Poems*. And he had shown me at various times the poems that were later published as *Love Poems*, as well as some longer poems for possible publication in *Evergreen Review*, *The New American Poetry*, and other projected collections. From correspondence with his contemporaries and from his own lists of poems for various proposed publications I was able to add most of the poems that fill out *The Collected Poems*.

But there remained many poems of which I had never heard, or doubted that he would have published without revising, ones that seemed too similar to other poems of the same period or were too fragmentary. In the course of restudying the manuscripts and collecting his correspondence, however, I came to realize that O'Hara at one time or another would most likely have published all of his poems, and that the present volume was the logical and necessary completion of their publication. (It is of course entirely possible that more unknown poems may yet come to light.)

Dates of composition from the manuscripts are given in brackets below the poems; undated poems are placed where any evidence suggests they belong.

I am greatly indebted to Robert Fizdale, Joan Mitchell, Lawrence Osgood, Larry Rivers, Ned Rorem, Ben Weber, and Mary E. Cooley (Secretary, The Hopwood Room, University of Michigan Library), and Mary E. Janzen (MSS Research Specialist, Special Collections, The Joseph Regenstein Library, University of Chicago) for copies of "lost" poems. And I am very grateful to Maureen O'Hara, John Ashbery, Bill Berkson, Zoe Brown, Margaret Cooley, Jane Freilicher, Mike Goldberg, David Kermani, Joseph LeSueur, Duncan MacNaughton, Merle Marsicano, Roger Shattuck, Alex Smith, Patsy Southgate and Anne Waldman for warmly appreciated assistance in preparing this volume for publication.

Donald Allen
1977/1996

Introduction
Bill Berkson

One is always eager to know more of the ins and outs and specific circumstances of Frank O'Hara's poems, including the relations between individual poems and others that they sometimes surprisingly connect to. The more complete the telling, it seems, the greater the mystery of detail. Just as O'Hara could write, "What is happening to me, allowing for lies and exaggerations which I try to avoid, goes into my poems"—a statement at once as mysterious and practical as there has ever been of the relation of poetry to experience—the poems make you curious about their occasions because they are so clear about what happens in them. Of course, as O'Hara also insisted, a poem is its own occasion, and between one poem and the rest, in the wide span of his poetic output, occasions and the poems that rise to them combine and refract in lifelike ways. "Poetry is life to me," after all, was another way of O'Hara's telling what went into his poems.

Many of the poems in *Poems Retrieved* are refractive with others in O'Hara's huge output, as the book itself is with the other compendious books that show his range, thematic, formal and otherwise. Types of poems occur both in and out of sequence; there are surges into new territory and doublings back. The editor Donald Allen's dedication of the book "For Edwin Denby who asked, 'And when will we have the *complete* poems of Frank O'Hara?'" suggests that, together with its companion volume *Early Writing*, which appeared concurrently under Allen's Grey Fox imprint in 1977, he meant both volumes of previously uncollected work to be hinged to the original *Collected Poems* until a new edition (complete, per Denby's urging) could be prepared. Lacking that, the three books stand together as representative of such completion.

Frank O'Hara once speculated that the entirety of William Carlos Williams's poetry was one continuous epic expressive of the man's existence. Similarly, even while returning regularly to the discrete [discretionary?] delights of one or another of O'Hara's poems, to imagine the whole run of them as bearing the logic of a unitary creation is helpful, too; it reinforces what one early lyric refers to as "this meaning growing," an articulation of the curiosity and necessity that bind one work to the next. Some of the pieces in *Poems Retrieved* are very slight—fragments, really. Others, especially the very early ones, feel overly convoluted in their rhetorical maneuverings. Yet none are false. Both *Early Writing* and *Poems Retrieved* have their drastic side; as ultimate retrievals, they bypass whatever reservations O'Hara himself might have had about seeing these largely unpublished and otherwise fugitive works in print, even in so candid a setting as each edition proposes. Whatever he may have felt about those poems, the fact is, he retained them. "Because you don't throw it away it is a poem," he said once when the issue came up of what to do with things that don't quite make the grade. Then, too, you can see why he never committed them to print and also why he kept them, because each has something in it distinctly worth keeping.

The retrievals that Donald Allen made of Frank O'Hara's poems began in 1968 with his sorting through the manuscripts of poetry and prose in cartons and files that Kenneth Koch took away for safekeeping in two suitcases from Frank's loft at 791 Broadway the night in July 1966 after Frank died—the nearly 700 items that first Kenneth and I and then Frank's sister Maureen and her husband at the time, Walter Granville-Smith, subsequently photocopied a few weeks later. Together with the versions already published in books, magazines and anthologies, these manuscripts formed the textual basis for what Donald Allen—Don, as I came to know him as a neighbor in Bolinas in the 1970s—would call, when it first appeared, in 1971, "the splendid palace known as *The Collected Poems of Frank O'Hara*." A pared-down volume, *The Selected Poems of Frank O'Hara*, also edited by Don, came out in 1974, followed the next year by the book of uncollected prose, *Standing Still and Walking in New York*. It was in the latter book that Don first used the term "retrieved."

Donald Allen and Frank O'Hara became friends during the planning stages of *The New American Poetry*, for which O'Hara served as one of the prime consultants and in which he shares pride of place, by dint of space allotted (fifteen poems on thirty-one pages), a close second to the inclusions of Charles Olson's poetry. Like Frank, Don had been with the U.S. Navy in the Pacific during World War II; after enlisting in 1941, he worked with Navy Intelligence, gathering codebooks and data from inter-rogations and captured soldiers' diaries. By 1957, as the main instigator and editor of *Evergreen Review*, he had printed some of O'Hara's most im-portant poems, including "Why I Am Not a Painter," "A Step Away from Them" and "In Memory of My Feelings," and O'Hara sought his advice on at least two books published in the mid-1960s, as well as two more projected collections that were left unrealized at his death. By no meager coincidence, Don began work on *The New American Poetry* in 1958, at just about the same time as *The New American Painting* exhibition, on which Frank had worked for the Museum of Modern Art starting in 1957, em-barked on its two-year tour of eight European cities. Following on *The New American Painting*'s status as the signal gathering of first- and second-generation abstract expressionists to travel overseas, Don claimed that the poets showcased in his book represented "the dominant movement in the second phase of our twentieth-century literature and already exerting strong influence abroad."

We do not respond often, really, and when we do it is as if a light bulb went off.
                                        —"Nature and the New Painting," 1954

The present *Poems Retrieved* follows the lead of the second, revised 1996 Grey Fox edition by comprising 214 poems, including two added to those already in the first: the 1952 satire "It's the Blue" and an alternate version of the poem from 1956 inspired by a Philip Guston painting. Each of those later additions furthers an understanding of the general culture O'Hara made for himself and the uses he put it to, all part of the biography of the work. The relation, for instance, between the title line "It's the Blue," a literal translation of the phrase "C'est l'azur" from André Breton's "Au re-gard des divinités," and the character "John Myers," the target of O'Hara's quatrains, may appear obscure until you recall that the actual John Bernard Myers, beside being a puppeteer and, as director of the Tibor de Nagy Gallery, the publisher of O'Hara's first book, also had been managing editor of the New York Surrealist magazine *View* and the main proponent of the idea that, for O'Hara's work and that of the poets of the New

York School generally, Surrealism was the main antecedent. (Myers, a man whose gushing definitiveness could hardly be kept in check, was also responsible, nearly a decade later, for foisting the infamous "school" label on the poets he published.) The situation becomes a little clearer once it's noted that *View* had published Breton's poem in Edouard Roditi's translation, accompanied by drawings by Arshile Gorky, in 1946. Indeed, the diction in O'Hara's poem, although more pointedly on the attack, stays close to Breton's sublime French extravagance ("my heart is a cuckoo for God").

In the two versions of the Guston poem, on the other hand, the diction is peculiarly mixed between formality ("To be always in vigilance away") and the vernacular ("So I had to break his wristwatch") that had by the mid-'50s become characteristic of O'Hara's poetry. The issue between the two may have been whether or not to unmix the modes of utterance, as well as where to make an ending. (I keep recalling a third version, my fantasy perhaps, that ends succinctly—and so perfectly for Guston's image—"a surface agitation of the waters/means a rampart on the ocean floor is falling".) The lines of the flush-left stanza O'Hara cancelled in one typescript (about the fate of "the bully who broke my nose") appear in the other as drop lines:

I hit him
> *it fell off*
>> *I stepped on it*

so he
> *will never again know*
>> *the time.*

Interestingly, this poem is one of two written on the same day (December 20, 1956) about pictures O'Hara looked at in the Museum of Modern Art, the other being *Digression on "Number 1," 1948*, which found its way into O'Hara's monograph on Jackson Pollock three years later. There the sea is "enough beneath the glistening earth/to bear me. . . ." Whichever poem came first, the distance in mood—emotionally catty-corner, so to speak— is significant: the Guston one is all reverie, the one on Pollock cleaves to the moment and ends with a vision of "the future/which is not so dark." The "I" in front of two separate paintings sees differently, markedly altered. In *Collected Poems*, Donald Allen placed the Pollock before the Guston, followed in turn by the well-known "Why I Am Not a Painter." Part of the interest in these art-inspired poems is the idea that whatever occurs to one in front of anything—a work of art or another person, for that matter—is not just a valid response, but probably the truest one.

This sense of someone in front of things extends to that of the poet himself before his poem, deciding, as he can, what happens there. Toward the end of the notes, probably from sometime in 1956, for a talk called "Design Etc.," O'Hara proposes the act of writing a possible poem (one that may yet become identifiable among those he actually did write) as well as defining what that poem won't be. In practice he envisions Design as a near-mythological force of

> *clearheaded-poetry-respecting objectivity, without which the most*
> *sublime and inspired love lyrics or hate-chants would just be muddy*
> *rantings. As the poem is being written, air comes in, and light, the form*
> *is loosened here and there, remarks join the perhaps too consistently*
> *felt images, a rhyme becomes assonant instead of regular, or avoided all*
> *together for variety and point, etc. All these things help the poem mean*
> *only what it itself means, become its own poem, so to speak, not the*
> *typical poem of a self-pitying or infatuated writer.*

The breadth of what Frank O'Hara took to be poetry is reflected in the many kinds of poems he wrote. The quick release from riveted (and riveting) attentiveness to direct response being his mission and métier, the rate of response, as well as the wide net cast by his attentions throughout, is extraordinary, as if the world would stop without his continually remarking on its activities. Turning the pages of any of his collections, you wonder what he didn't turn his hand to, what variety of poem he left untried or didn't, in some cases, as if in passing, anticipate.

I see my vices
lying like abandoned works of art
which I created so eagerly
to be worldly and modern
and with it

About Frank O'Hara's earliest writings John Ciardi, whose workshops O'Hara took at Harvard, recalls: "He showed his brilliance rather than his feelings. That was a point I often made in talking about his writing. I think, in fact, it was when he used his brilliance to convey rather than to *hide behind* that he found his power." What John Ashbery calls O'Hara's "period of testing" continued for some time beyond his student years, and, sensibly enough, a good three-quarters of *Poems Retrieved* is taken up with poems dating from that time (roughly 1950–1954), after which anything he wrote was less prone to fall short of the mark. As late as 1952 in New York, he is still signing poems with his Hopwood Award pen name "Arnold Cage." The run-of-the-mill poem of this period is liable to feature an array of theatrical posturings, all the while betraying the intent of summoning, by way of letting an adopted artificial language play out, consistencies of real wit and eloquence. Part of O'Hara's youthful testing was his willingness to try out, beside a slew of poetic personae, any available forms and genres: accordingly, among the poems here are epigrams (many of those spot-on), eclogues, calligrams, sestinas, sonnets, quatrains and tercets and rhymed couplets, birthday poems and envois, poems in prose, one-liners and lines of great mystery and beauty ("Sentimentality, aren't you sunset?" "Do you know what the phiz really/looks like?"). There are fragments that stay fragments and have a kind of inviolable strength, like bits of antique parchment, of the fragment as such. The more extraneous early poems tend toward bumpy rides accelerated by mock exclamations and questions that go nowhere, along with nasty arty quips and fripperies that echo Frank's readings in *amuse-bouche* modernists like Ronald Firbank and Ivy Compton-Burnett. What is striking, however, is the sheer number of such poems and their earthier counterparts—how intent he was, by way of experiment traditional and otherwise, on working through to the "tough heart of art," the "real right thing"—and also how attuned he was to the existential stakes involved. Meanwhile, the method in such silliness as some of the poems proclaimed—the seriousness with which O'Hara was already protecting his gift "from mess and measure"—would be apparent to anyone used to the drab alternatives of self-seriousness and pretense as normally (then as now) rampant in the officialese of American poetry.

As Kenneth Koch recalled, the poems of Frank's he first read in the early fifties were "sassy, colloquial and full of realistic detail"; realistic, one might add, because so quick to register the gists of the going styles:

> We loved our bodies,
> navyblue sneakers
>> Frank Sinatra
>>> and pistachio frappes,
> it's all in our heart and dirtied there

The later fifties, by comparison, show all the same qualities combined with a new assurance as to how they go together, which allows for the candor of

> What I really love is people, and I don't much care whom
> except for a few favorites who fit, which you understand.
> It's like the sky being above the earth. It isn't above
> the moon, is it? Nor do I like anyone but you and you.

and:

> if there were no cameras
> I would not know this boy
> but hatred becomes beauty anyway
> and love must turn to power or it dies.

By 1956, the year O'Hara turned 30, pretty much all the archness and other signs of struggle towards being, in Rimbaud's classic phrase, "absolutely modern" were abandoned in discovering an originality so "with it" in his own regard as to leave outside determinations behind. Not that posturing was gone, but that he had realized the postures appropriate for him and the poems. The work, with its various turns of autobiographical patter and declaration, had become, as John Ashbery put it, "both modest and monumental, with something basically usable about it." Right before the reader's eyes, so to speak, diverse textures of feeling come into focus in the imaginary present tense of another person's energetic consciousness:

> *Why are there flies on the floor*
> *in February, and the snow mushing outside*
> *and the cats asleep?*
> > *Because you came*
> *back from Paris, to celebrate your return.*

San Francisco, 2012

POEMS RETRIEVED

Noir Cacadou
or the Fatal Music of War

We were standing around
with guitars and mandolins
when the war ended. Yes.

The sea was calm and pale.
Almost polite. Whatever
had it meant to us, what

will you mean to me, does
nothing end? It was dull
as a spider's banquet. Just

twangings and a wave or
two. "Japee!" someone called
through his high red beard

and the Admiral said "Men
you were admirable." We
loved him as I love you. More,

and it meant nothing, simply
a remark after another war.
We were gay, we had won, we

dressed in stovepipes and
danced the measure of being
pleased with ourselves. That is

why I want you, must have
you. Draw the black line where
you want it, like a musical

string it will be love and lovely
and level as the horizon from
our exotic and dancing deck.

Your beard will grow very
fast at sea and you will
not know what instrument

you are patting. It will mean
a lot to you until the lines
stop vibrating and become

a thin black cry that ends.
But no admiral will speak
yet, we've a lot to do first.

I'm not ready for my costume.
We'll beat the gong, yell
out our uneatable tongues,

wallow lasciviously in arms.
You'll see how easily we
provoke the waves, although

the sextant shakes and positions
get difficult. And every dawn
the whine will go up, the black

look that means love is near.
We'll draw our own lines
and be what the sea tries

to talk about. Then afterwards
we'll help each other dress, lay
flowers at the dummy's feet.

A Doppelgänger

Do you mean that
my gaze is not a look
and my clothes decide
like a Delacroix banner
what will happen to-
morrow although they
are quite foreign to me
hide thoughtful flesh?

Do you mean that
my yellow hair like
thrashing wheat hangs
wild over my forehead
and blue limpets peer
above my cheekbones
Rilkean discoveries?

Do you mean that
one fierce hand drags
by a thumb from my
appendix while the
other photographs old
ladies and my black
eyes roll and swagger
down Washington Street?

Or do you mean that
my head is too high
I throw my plate about
the restaurant talk
too loud and bounce
the balls of my feet
my own worst enemy?

is it any of these my
friends you visit when
you think you think of me?

[Ann Arbor, November 1950]

Poem

Green things are flowers too
and we desire them more than
George Sand's blue rose not
that we don't shun poison oak

but if it's a question of loco
weed or marijuana why how
can we not rush glad and wild
eyes rolling nostrils flaring

towards ourselves in an unknown
pasture or public garden? it's
not the blue arc we achieve
nor the nervous orange poppy at

the base of Huysmans' neck
but the secret chlorophyll
and the celluloid ladder hid-
den beneath the idea of skin.

[Ann Arbor, November 1950]

Entombment

The wind is cold and echoes a banshee
off the red wall that peers into cemeteries.
And the yellow hearses arrive, laden
with nails and pikestaffs for decoration

of the alabaster bier into which your
rivulets of tears still eat their seams.
Poor shroud! that will be pleated by
the first dallying wind, thus unprotected

thus glamorized. "Anything worth having
is worth throwing away" they taught in
the synagogues and though He took rope
to their backsides they did not shut up.

Now they stand paling into a future
which will melt their crosses, caught
by the fish in their throats, gargoyles
themselves. Their cocks drop off. They cry.

[November 1950]

6

A Slow Poem

I wonder if you can die of
sadness   What a way to go

A split-leaved plant bulges
out of the gloomy fireplace

and the three wide windows
are embarrassed by darkness

A few objects project themselves
into a sinister scatter, just

a corkscrew a can opener
a pen knife but all lethal

And my books and pictures
yearn toward me mentally as if

they were toys or games while
I stare at this green ceiling

And whine helplessly of
sadness   What a way to go

In Gratitude to Masters

to Professor Roy Cowden

Sonnet

As the learned snow falls lightly on trees
and obscures them, seeming fragile at first,
intellectuality's modest thirst
embellishes its coronation frieze

upon human aspirations. And lest
the icy sun burn naked up the roots
this music through the whining wind so mutes
flailing gales that we are safe and seem best

to ourselves despite ambiguities,
for may we not call down protecting skies
at will? not blind, not rigid and screaming

may we not beg from subtlety's dreaming
light our lack? Finding in art that strength snow
clears, warming the barren earth, roots, fallow.

Envoi

Thus to the Professor
fly our small hands, not
spilling the soul to a confessor
nor in a mold caught

nor in training for flight.
But he leads us to the light,
there where it so naturally
falls upon the unknown sea.

Poem

Suppose that grey tree, so nude
and desperate,

              began to waltz
slowly in time to something we
are deaf to in the thickening snow.

Would it be merely trying to get
warm and true,

              as it seems one
does while dancing,

                   or would this be
an invitation from the inanimate
world our bones,

              trying not to ache
with foreboding, seemed to warn us of
in early childhood?

Then, unenlightened by desire and
satisfied by very real dreams, we
were able briefly,

                as from a window,
to look bravely upon the baroque will
of objects,

              not knowing, in our clever
smile,

          who really felt the cold.

Poem

Poised and cheerful the
squirrel moves in the grey
tree passing upward into
the world's leafy aerial
away from us and eager for
the infinite

            berry his
volatile eye rolls shyly
comprehensive and sees
us as specks in a corner
midway between the dull
earth and birds' rare
nests now

           empty forever
fading into wider sky
leaves are all below
him wires farther from
each other our antennae
no longer conduct him
cold and gone

              oh squirrel
why didn't you tell us
you knew how to get there!

Song

I'm going to New York!
(what a lark! what a song!)
where the tough Rocky's eaves
hit the sea. Where th'Acro-
polis is functional, the trains
that run and shout! the books
that have trousers and sleeves!

I'm going to New York!
(quel voyage! jamais plus!)
far from Ypsilanti and Flint!
where Goodman rules the Empire
and the sunlight's eschato-
logy upon the wizard's bridges
and the galleries of print!

I'm going to New York!
(to my friends! mes semblables!)
I suppose I'll walk back West.
But for now I'm gone forever!
the city's hung with flashlights!
the Ferry's unbuttoning its vest!

[New York, January 1951]

A Pathetic Note

Think of all the flowers you've ever seen
and remember me to my mother, or be kind

to some white-haired blue-eyed old lady
who might remind me of Grandaunt Elizabeth

were I with you. When you go down West
Fourteenth Street think of Africa and me,

why don't you? and be careful crossing
streets. Keep photographing the instant

so that in my hysteria I will know what
it is like there; and while my teeth rot and

my eyes seem incapable of the images I'd
hoped, I will know you are at least all right.

While I write this eleven windows stare,
clothes hanging on the wall stir testily.

The ceiling's miles away. I'm sitting on
the floor. Since I last saw you things

are worse. What can I do without love,
without honor, without fame? Can you see

me? It is evening. Other people's lights
are going on, I think. But not your friend's.

[New York, January 1951]

Poem

Just as I leave the theatre
you come in the door. Or I

receive a letter saying you
are a policeman. My day retches

amidst its studies and you
are rigid with hauteur for

months. But then by expert
montage, a mountain growing

out of a diamond, the same
principle, you appear before me.

I spill your whiskey: you are
beautiful! When my back is

turned you still love me.
Mirrors go blind in our flame.

[New York, February 1951]

Windows

This space so clear and blue
does not care what we put

into it   Airplanes disappear
in its breath and towers drown

Even our hearts leap up when
we fall in love with the void

the azure smile the back of a
woman's head and takes wing

never to return   0 my heart!
think of Leonardo who was born

embraced life with a total eye
and now is dead in monuments

There is no spring breeze to
soften the sky   In the street

no perfume stills the merciless
arc of the lace-edged skirt

[Ann Arbor, February 1951]

A Byzantine Place

1 At a Mondrian Show

How excited I am!   My piggy
heart is at a traffic intersection

However I run a mirror slaps
me in the face   I'm not tired

of being told I'm beautiful yet
Shall I ever be that ghost of

a chance the right money on
the right nose   Our portraits

hang restlessly and kick their
feet while we run around alas!

2 My Face in the Street

That I must do these things
for you find the fortunate bird
and kill where he flies so strong

is there any simple event this
does not answer?   As still
oh my people as still life I'm
your bowl of bread and your
black thought   Do not question
me   Sustain my panic my grope

3 A Sketch of Mallarmé

They're not funny
the unfled flights
the unlaughed laughs
the eye on the beach

that's forever awash
and I can no longer
snigger, Ted, as when
you gave me the picture

then it was easier
only the flesh was sad
and these white silences
hadn't pinned me down

It's for ever I write
because the struggle may
knock the breath out of me
I want someone to know

4 A Program for Music

Have you heard music
that's like a hand around
the heart a lace hand?

not a maker or pusher
but an unzipping of images
in the vulgar grottos

an essential passion
that ignores no tear or whim
and addresses the hobbyhorse

as elegantly as the bridge
and cries beware the blue sky
sometimes love gets lost

5 The Naked Element

Move the mountains
over closer
              I intend
to dance if I wish

I climb on pierstakes
higher eagles
              to love
in an airplane of clouds

and we do wingdings
on the wind
              get bloody
rolling over stars

it's all in your heart
and here
              if I please
you are all my love

[Ann Arbor, February 1951]

Lines Across the United States

The night's getting black
The train is cold
My back aches already

I don't want to smoke
We're going too fast
Our windows hurt the air

Last night I was sick
And this morning worse
I threw my self into this coach

The wheels slice quickly
The rails do struggle
The mirrors shake like puddles

I'm sitting all night
I didn't buy a pillow
My watch got broken last week

I've not done much
I've loved too little
And I'm tired of running

[Between New York & Ann Arbor,
March 1951]

An Epilogue: To the Players of *Try! Try!*

1 John Ashbery

If I get sick you'll fly
to me, John, and not eat dinner
on the plane for sheer worry.

If it's night the red lights
will affright you of my blood letting,
and your verse will flood

with memories of all those
choral compositions on prison themes
we both have so enjoyed.

Indeed, my health will fail
in apprehension for your nerves, then
rally to greet you strongly.

The words I write for your voice
will always, I hope, resound as your own
lilting and agate love of ears.

2 Jack Rogers

Not lissome and not
gruntingly wholesome, your

humor's a Rasputin of emphasis,
Jack, a charade in front of

Mother Superior, the sub-
stantial unwillingness to

charm that frightens our
giggles into eager screeches!

Your grin across a room
makes me draw a sabre to

charge my nearest and
dearest friend for the fun

of it! And your voice in
my typewriter attempts to

tease the wit out of serious
situations, so we won't be

wrong goosing psychiatrists
for the sake of our guts.

3 Violet Lang

Image of all felinities
and Grand Lady of the
turnpikes, in decadent verse
you'd be a giantess but I,
in good health, exclaim you
mine! and speak familiarly.

Dancer always, to me, and
tea room's despaired-of voyou,
you are my Bunny and other
people's Violet, a saint of
circumstance and the dangerous
Birthday Party. I quote you
back to yourself in all women
and love you as if *Symposium*
had not been writ in jest.

Kiss me. We'll never again fight
in a cafeteria of friends. I want
your voice in my ear so the sun
will be hotter, and as Bermudas
make us dizzy we'll clamber over
mountains as red and yellow as
clowns, shouting to John and Jack:
"Hurry up! Poo, poo! Tra la!"

Poem

I can't wait for spring!
this year — dare I say it?
I'm ready, I'll grab and
hold, roll over and over
in the sweet bulbs, smell
of dirt and musk and
nectar and air, and then
I'll leap erect as any
adolescent reading sweet
Petronius into that
ravishing! raving! that
blue blue sky!
                    O soave fanciulla!

[Ann Arbor, March 1951]

21

Poem

This vessel I've chosen
is a zebra in the open

so quick to the finger
and curiously limber

whenever my dreams' eyes
conceal all courses

a flashing uncertainty
floods my caprices

only by hazardous
pain can I choose

tears I am still crying
wake my tired rowing

Voyage à Paris

What's the sense
of going to Paris
if you're not going to be
the Eiffel Tower?

If Cleopatra
has had a breast
removed, watch out!
but feel for yourself.

I don't love
the widespread rise on
precipitate winds,
my strut's a thumb-

your-nose, my ribs? hah!
my feet in a meadow of stars
hear spherical music.
None of your elevators!

I will climb the Seine.
And the Nile. The world's
a baseball in your mitt,
in my fingers a balloon.

O tour Eiffel, o clouds,
o Egypt, you're not tired!

[Ann Arbor, March 1951]

A Party Full of Friends

Violet leaped to the piano
stool and knees drawn up
under her chin commenced to
spin faster and faster sing-
ing "I'm a little Dutch boy
Dutch boy Dutch boy" until
the rain very nearly fell
through the roof!
                         while, from
the other end of the room,
Jane, her eyeballs like the
crystal of a seer spattering
my already faunish cheeks
with motes of purest colored
good humor, advanced slowly.

"Poo!" said Hal "they are
far too elegant to be let
off the pedestal even for a
night" but Jack quickly and
rather avariciously amended
"it's her birthday," then
fell deliberatively silent
as
   Larry paced the floor. Oh
Larry! "Ouch" he cried (the
latter) "the business isn't
very good between Boston and
New York! when I'm not paint
ing I'm writing and when I'm
not writing I'm suffering

for my kids I'm good at all
three"
        indeed you are, I
added hastily with real ad-
miration before anyone else
could get into the poem, but
Arnie, damn him! had already
muttered "yes you are" not
understanding the fun of
idle protest.
            John yawked
onto the ottoman, having eyes
for nought but the dizzy
Violet, and George thought
Freddy was old enough to
drink. Gloria had not been
invited, although she had
brought a guest.
                What
confusion! and to think
I sat down and caused it
all! No! Lyon wanted some
one to give a birthday
party and Bubsy was born
within the fortnight the
only one everybody loves. I
don't care. Someone's going
to stay until the cows
come home. Or my name isn't

            Frank O'Hara

                    [Ann Arbor, April 1951]

A Curse

Let all poison accrues to
him exist in the violet, oh
      special to me!

and there flourishing let
poison be blood to the pig
      who wears pants!

for that flower is mine will
banish hurt from my heart as
      he falls to root

and rain waters strength from
his limbs free my muscles my
      admiring eyes, bah!

let the fever rots me enrich
his maggots my halo strangle
      his niggardly heart!

[Ann Arbor, April 1951]

A Portrait

1
The sun sits heavily on
the red flowers and upon
the boy who sits beside
them and on the vines rattling
against the boy's pink ear
and upon the flowing water,
the plashing thoughts, the
clouds hailing and farewelling
that incendiary face. In

the midst of concrete water's
most insipid, thought tends
to take a dive, no elevator;
there's no awning for the heart.

2
"I always did think
in the crib of home, o
my Dardanella! that I
was one of those ones

who left sharp toys
in their daddies' beds
in their mummies' towels
and got the maids fired

who hoarded dark spiders
in their brothers' socks
in their sisters' paintboxes
and blamed best friends

who ran away from town
when their aunt was sick
when their cousin was waked
and flirted with cops.

Now now now Dardanella!
don't say goodbye to me.
I sing better now I'm older
I'm absconding with girls!"

3
However the mounting wail of adolescence crashes
upon the amusement park he is not confused, the boy,

he is not discountenanced by any number of silences
or natural events like bombs. "Be mine some day!" he

admonishes automobiles and palatial residences
as well as the ocean and Catholicism. When he barks

up the wrong tree he pretends to despise flagpoles
and all that is stylish or dear, is "we moderns."

He beats upon Love a merciless tattoo, burrows his
three-day stubble into those white thighs, and She

perforce, depressed, must have a breast removed.
He was never really a child? exostosis! excelsior!

4
To th' expanse of the moon
and to Brooklyn's jewels
he croons his winning shot:

"I've sat up all day, nobody
has been by. Me without a
balalaika or cowboy brother!

Still hot from the stunning
sun, come get me stranger!
My lips are moist with playgrounds,

little girls've touched my
knees. And all the stars, when
I look up, are on my eyes."

[Ann Arbor, May 1951]

Mr. O'Hara's Sunday Morning Service

There is this to be said
for Sunday morning: that if
I have been very bad the night
before and wake up feeling

like a drab on a sunny day,
Dick will pop into my room
and invite me out to the
high abandoned airfield.

There, the sun will seem
properly chilly and the wind
will not compromise us
with any silly sentiment

I will walk about on the
heaving grass rather shakily
and observe the model airplanes
lofted by dry blue currents.

As Dick like a discus hurler
throws his wood into the sky
I begin to feel engaged and
follow the glider straining

its little spirit into swoops
that clumsily break and bounce
to earth with a grunt. Then
he must pick up its wings

and go home, to make repairs,
to putty its nose and straighten
its tail, to talk about winds
and temperatures and balance,

to think about theories of
flight, and shave perhaps. So
all through dinner our clear
anxious eyes remain aloft.

[Ann Arbor, May 1951]

The Soldier

Marching into the crouching sun
I'm humming death's Arab songs
bending my back under bottles or
sneering the smiles from little girls

Oh god! I tear up pictures and throw
my books out the window like a nun
in heat the blood forces through
my hands and feet and head and groin

Like a crazed dog that hears someone
else's trumpet I go yapping after pals
and cannot bear to pant alone for
I can imagine how the hermit dies

Or on a mountain howling for the
hamper of gin I'm sick of sick Manfred
and the clouds I cry you all to hurry
up here where I'm flogged by eagles

[Ann Arbor, May 1951]

Parties

Do you know what the phiz really
looks like? the anchovy eye
unrolled and without blemish
without a handkerchief at parties

Or is it that our hearts don't
really listen to Dietrich? the mirror
has a streak across its face as
if a cake of soap had slipped

And the candles tremble perhaps
with lust perhaps simply because
they are cold anyhow they know
everyone we've been to bed with

Open the ventilator open the door
the sky is peering through the
Venetian blinds Kenny you're having
a wonderful party but I am dying

In the middle of a martini in
the middle of a dance oh don't
ask me to clean up the place no
tomorrow no airplanes just flies

[In the Street of Children the Sun Is Cold]

In the street of children the sun is cold
and the winter accepts leaves for prizes,
autos roar into the plate-glass praises
which the meanest faces muster and hold,
loving themselves most.
                              The little girl's doll
farts into a heady wind and steam shrieks
to get out, and of the cracks and the creaks
and the dark stares of the cop in the hall.

Yellowing into an orient's lapse
of life they fiddle with each other, no
fooling and no fun, while the sun gallops

into another street to start trouble
which no child can die fast enough to know:
love dies in the bright praise of its double.

[Ann Arbor, May 1951]

Form and Utterance

The barking dog kisses the red fireplug.
And tries to smile. The fireplug is too strong,
not fooled by "that dumb affectionate pug."
The pug feels quite irrelevant. So long.

Beside our bored friend a bay milk horse stands.
The dog has minced away. The fireplug sneers.
The wind is very warm in June. "No hands
upon my reins guide me through city fears;

I could love a monkey" moans the dull horse.
Where is that interesting dog? Our red friend
stares at penthouses and whistles. A hearse
wanders suggestively by. It's the end!

[Ann Arbor, May 1951]

Round Objects

Stolen into by vended guises
the marmalade jar swells and,
withdrawn, becomes a lark. There

in the field it skills with flowers
and a traffic painted like the sun
rolls towards our vise over clovers,

fourleaf, tripe. In Jamaica, was it?
a turbine full of oranges, land for
much ado. The jazz was simple, and

only in our heavy language furrows
of shank must its dart assume
pre-Adamic clarity. Let us

rest in the grasses, covered with scented
bugs. Sand admires the perfect vamp
and lip, the tractor reels the sum.

[Ann Arbor, June 1951]

Sky Rhymes

If we are one
in a single sun
the stars below
are weeping snow

our head is wheeling
without ever feeling
the interstellar
mirror Dweller

the blind earth rolling
under His strolling
's an axial log
in a cloudless bog

      the Milky Way
      is not very gay
      a thickening path
      a cool foot-bath

[Ann Arbor, June 1951]

The Air and Sex of Early Day

Your breath wakes me like a bolt from the blue:
the gingko tree is suddenly cautious
its rising leaves become unanimous
and I, dear, am setting my sail for you.

Although our waves may beat the children, Pooh
and Alice, into little scrofulous
stones and lichen, interesting dolls to us
(I never pat them slap them nor do you)

and the wake of our loving riptide, fun!
drowns out the clatter of leaves on windows
quenches our eyes (the gingko reminder)

sings to the kids that are happy willows
weeps and loves both of them like a dead son,
I lose nothing: not a leaf! and find you.

[New York, August 1951]

A Virtuoso

The crowd is assembled in decorous rows
like flowers outside a rich zoo. He
strides from the wings, the black aviator,
sits down and bats out a Concert Adagio
and Rondo! flailing octaves in a great
grill of black crosshatches across
the proscenium. Monkeys appear and
clamber seriously up this trellis of
atonal spears. Like tin-hatted hydrogen
workers, they clap, the dopy audience,
but he's not through. With a fierce glance
of irrelevance he jams his elbow up
the sounding box's warm dessert: a soprano
from his childhood screams with child
and dashes her brains out against
the sole of his foot that's pedalling
madly up hill! And while millions of
rosebuds fall from our pianist's aching
hammers nobody thinks of anything but
those clattering bleeding teeth.

[New York, August 1951]

38

A Classical Last Act

1

We are beginning everything and forgetting
freshly, as audience to standing room insights

and willingnesses that accrue to foreign
tongues, music and demagoguery. Hazard

and lapis lazuli are co-stars as the booming
curtain shoots up and down for the final

twin times. For the interim we are priming
the pump of forgetting, tears and lavalieres,

the throttling of all extraneous decoration
in favor of emotional impertinence and

structural wailing, to be not so dry as bone
and not so facile as an artesian well.

Bang! bang! bang! and it is just like the
subway: we've at last found an empty car,

open doors are swaying for miles ahead, and
the conductor's in a perfect tantrum, eh?

2

"I love yuh!" screams the dying man
as his sockets grow black and his lips

fall to bleeding with foam under sky.
Quaking and shivering at hell's fire

the nearing sun beckons from behind
the man, the shout is still "I love yuh!"

as if the dense opal shiftings of shore
or the passively snickering wavelets

gave a rap. It's all in front of
purely itinerant clouds, the forever individual

who never loan each other accent or shape.
And he shouts again so his voice can change

words, so the scenery will notice him, the
analogous excitements of his breath, our death.

[New York, October 1951]

The Ideal Bar

The jasmine blinker of your breath
opposed across the bar your whiskey eyes
and the miserable distances only stank
for thumbsucking zebras and poilus.

We were the pink chair of plush
rolling its tongue to the window, night,
and the bastards who lived below
the hall. It was in line for our scratches

and for the bellyaches of venery. The
smile, the same smile for the management
as for the Sixtine putti, sand towards
the dark corner's secret peopled incense.

The music floated from discs of
beery autumn in gardens and promenades,
the soul of the Kermesse: your pure
eyes which flared the void my heart fed.

The Painter's Son

(Joe Rivers)

The impetuous purple success
the slap of brush or blob
wander off the canvas sky
at a scowl from the fierce dark boy

and the meddling with real
lives, art as midwife and lech,
pestilential singing
beside the bed of whirling flowers

all the illuminations, warfares,
whirligigs and
troglodytic rites, don't
escape this kunst-clubbing prattler

all fragilities wreck like
bicycles when he takes over
but! his bony fists splinter
beautifully on the tough heart of art.

[New York, November 1951]

A Military Ball

Valuably, the tune unwinds us! with, ah!
its brash formality and its melancholy echoes
of vulgarity. We are swept fast about by winds,
loving the surprise of sudden power over
each burning waltzer of the body's parade, tenting
tonight inside the bunting carrousel.

Rollicking with laughter at pretty things
and not even regretting our rompers as
naked we dance towards the silliness of our pain,
not acknowledging the boom and buzz of the band, the
endless explosion of its music, or the easy toss of
your and my heart on the baize, the ocean, the sward.

Love blooming in bombardment this is, dear,
all we know before we fall to silent wars: Violet,
not the glamor of your uniform by mine, but these
game convolutions on your voice above the dark.

[New York, November 1951]

42

Poem

"Green oboes!" the parrot cries,
and why wouldn't he? hasn't the Master
linked them to perfumes?

A sudden rush of recorded music
makes the child on the rusting fire escape
back towards the fire

screaming, though a million fingers
glitter at his fatty throat rapturously.
Turned down, we whine,

Schumann and I. The pitch of autumn
is too high, the trees tear off arpeggios
as if they were cuff links.

Must we summer voyages and hear festivals,
sun looming always larger and over the sill?

[1951]

43

Serenade

Starlings are singing
like glass breaking
and falling into a rather
vulgar plate. Somewhere
a nightingale waits for each
of us, crying its heart
out.

      Oh I don't know, say,
say it's your fingernails
scratching down my neck
with a fragile roar.

                  No,
it's starlings singing,
simply starlings singing.
And all around us pieces
of a great sad hero, yes,
an eagle had him by the balls.
Doves are still crying.
Starlings hide, my love,
in the eaves. Good night.

Vernissage Jane Freilicher

The bell jars the white walls
and a wind sweeping the plains
of Central America smashes
a hydraheaded fiery screaming
beast onto the rocks by
the sea. The clarity of mist
roars, its paean of life's swart
intelligibility through legend,
need, must, pitch, risable ague.
Bewildered and indeed in tears
we do well to be snotty, our
eyes drowning in hand-me-downs
and glycerine, a few klieg lights
under the faltering chin, and
a city of ants for a navel.
We have striven, dear one,
and yet. But today's sun
streams like a midnight harpist
across the islands of artistic
weariness, that bud of sweetness
which the sailors bit, and stayed.

Shelter

Blows descend upon the rock
ricocheting into ears like a piano
and there are tears and jobations

everywhere.
Between each blast of the bazookas
we fall into a valley of silence

where the blood audibly drips
from ventricle to vial
under the red cross of our society.

Some read novels about Hyacinth
or Hamilcar, and others, equally cagy,
watch the sky flood with germs.

If we cry before the UN Building's
enigmatic mirror, brave sentiments
crush us in their orchestra arms—

but on this wailing cliff, love,
you are only my burrowing instrument.
and I am a fox in a hole.

Schoenberg

In a fever of style, having slaughtered the false Florimells
of harmonious thought and their turgid convincements, he
marshalled lightning and the beautiful stench of singed clouds.
Some sneered: him a silly Quixote! but he laid waste Central
Europe and painted with the salt of Jenghiz the wounds of World
War I. Not enough women rubbed their breasts against trees while
waiting for big nightingales, so he pushed these ladies, intelligent
refugees from Weimar, into a Pierrot-less sea, and everywhere the
frontiers of a sensibility whose left foot was only then fearfully
emerging trembled like the rim of the sun under his hot clothes.
The classic grace of a spirit resting on broken glass informed the
shell of his virgin Muse with pink echoes from the newspapers,
at the mercy of every fresh breath from the tradewinds.

[It Is a Weak Cold Morning and I Roll]

It is a weak cold morning and I roll
in bed. The black chest's empty of
its liquor and last night has wandered
off like an intellectual. I peer
at the paper and your face growls back,
yes. Your death will not change
the conspiracies, but you'll become
another kind of rage. The semi-everythings
will discover your grapes and nibble,
discriminating that you also painted,
just like William Blake. And it won't
be lost on them, they are too greedy
and too mean.

Poem

The tough newspaper boy will wear
a stripe and a scar on his ass
for this kiss I give you tonight
is tomorrow's, your bun and beard.

Are you aware that snow's flying
from the heat of my eyes about
your touchy feet? You may tremble
but not shake clear, poor fir,

and if I could be compassionate
as a horse you'd hate my whinny,
try to trap me in blue meadows
like the stallion across the street

who's a sucker for clover. Pearl
of the Indian floor and black H
above my heart, why do you always
whine and drunkenly sob, telephone,

catch me in your cloud as if
we were high on a hill? Over there
the sun is burning up, and you
wonder what land this is, what love.

On a Friend's Being Insulted

Would wish and again that you sidle
through the green light of twenty five
this warfare, these coins, this this,
cobalt lizard of gristle, brrrrrrrrrrr
from islands other, who must
snort if we're to thrive.
                              That old
chatter strums like blood on
ice cubes and would come amucker
surf. If it were free. Shake out
the lice of words like a banner
through the ferrying air as
roars the flame of our together.

To Dick

The Holy Ghost appears
to Wystan in Schrafft's
to me in the San Remo
wearing a yellow sweater.

Ghost couples, gathers, sweeps
and lashes and crashes like
wave on shingle! is blonde.
The sky opens. Such choirs

with their entangling moods
rush us, more subway than
opera, into an airdrome
filled with Palm trees and Eyes.

[New York, January 1952]

The Puritan

"The eye vomits
to think of it
and the gun trembles
in my hand! That,
that quivering sky
and the smiling bird
like a festering window!
Do not invite me!"

The finger twitches.
To go to bed, and be
in love, is to shoot
the same bird slower
than with a stranger.

"Fly to Africa!
Learn Eskimo!
At least seek someone
with an air of redolence,
yellow eyes, or a breath
ripened in garlic!"

A Romantic Poet to His Muse

The monks in the temple garden
whisper, and nightingales slit
each others' throats, the many
tongued to death. A trumpet

bursts into night, announcing
no war but our eternal hate.
The lady who lifts her window
to the ominous silence of lust

streams blood from her fingers
and is dumb with the beauty
of her being. Like a moon
plunging in the New Guinea ocean

her heart moans unceasingly
for the knife, bursts upwards
and is stilled only by the talons
of a ferreting bat. I must

save her, although I am mad
from their prayers, and each
nightingale has dropped a tender
breast upon my thighs, in death.

[New York, January 1952]

52

A Greek Girl at Riis Beach

The girl fishes up the sea.
A tube beside her holds the pole
and she tugs the ribbon, dirty
ribbon holding her and then
tumbling jet hair falls into wind
flashing with the sun's rays,
the stinging tails and arrows
of the jumping rabid ocean.

Red skirt blows up to nipples
and she lunges her pole over
the scared sea, flailing and rushing
retreating waves, terrified faces
of the little white dogs. Her eyes
in their wilderness gather fishes,
dreaming salmon leap over cheekbones
into the hot spring of her blood
and her lips, wet with the flavor
and the subtle scales, glitter
against the horizon. Birds flush
from her sweating palms. aieeeeeee!
barracuda! tarpon! ray!

Mounting the sandy mare, rearing!
throbbing legs astride she gallops
into a furious sunset whose fire
is quenched by the prodigality
of fishers who fly the seas.

[New York, January 1952]

Poets up in the Air

after Roger de la Fresnaye

The apples on the leaves
swing in their dulcet maroons
and a sparrow flocks alone
into white tunnels of wind
beyond the giant's azure stubbed chins.

Over the hill like a snood
kine lope, hunting heavily
beneath the pear trees; a tiger
copulates with the fancy ewes
that escape from a Ford pickup, severally,

and there are the strangers,
nearer, the millions of ants digging
happily on a dry bosom, bees
crop the clover with rhinestone
teeth. A zeppelin muses over, smiling.

And it doesn't have to be
spring, the wind opens like a glass
door. John and I, sitting at canasta,
rise into redwhiteblue helicopter clouds,
being that giant's darlings, some scenery for the mass.

[New York, February 1952]

[I Walk Through the Rain]

I walk through the rain
and it's really piling up tonight.
My head like a bullet
pierces the downpour.

She in a dark window
irons some man's shirt
with ponderous columns
atop which the sleepy eggplants
shine in the moon of her peering
out at the mysterious night,

and that's me.
Why must my eyes, pleading,
response the sky's convulsion,
humble me before a domestic shrine,
obscure, lonely, slow,
as if I needed this stranger?

[New York, February 1952]

Chanty

Such that! to be done: killingness,
rascality, personification leaves me
dippy. And it is to when as to what
like all the other boys my age and

moreover. If to be dead to be be,
is not our favorite airplane "Shalimar"
the ever rudderless and tawny?
to be fed only once a day and irregularly?

Never been the type for much horseplay
serious as a lady's handbag, muscled
and intent on the high water mark:
Aoua! let not that old devil start to rise.

[New York, February 1952]

56

Grace and George, an Eclogue

Grace and George are showing themselves some scenery and history. The Alps are rising under them like escalators and their blonde hair is tossing in the waves of an advancing sea of problems which, having been faced yesterday, seem only to have grown bolder. They have a very sweet attitude toward each other as if to say, "Well here we are," which however you will never hear that pair say, not if you listen by the hundreds.

Grace: Must you insist on wearing my old clothes! I thought that at least when you got out of the army finally you'd look a little less tacky.

George: Why are you always thinking about "the" war? Look about you: why must you always distrust the ease and variety of the adjacent hills, whose volcanic inundations you claim are too insistent, and peremptorily and characteristically you say they deny the fatal scowl which appears like a mud pack on the French face of what haunts us as beauty?

Grace: I saw the waning tulip of night fade into a gossamer shroud. I was all alone, and in that state you, suddenly as it were and especially if no thought is already in your mind, appreciate the particularity of all-ness and why it is always coupled with human singularity in cosmic regularity.

(Sings:) I wander, you wondereth, that she doth roam.
          In loneliness my sinecure and my abode.
          I have not set my skirts upon the path of fame.

The moon has meanwhile really come out as if summoned. The sea wrenches at its moorings as in a geodetic survey chart held over a candle flame, and edelweiss all around George and Grace, there on the breathless slopes, scream their thin-drawn wire voices until their eyes pop out a glittering blue of three-year-olds pierced by arrows at summer camps. On the floor of the star-strewn lake where a million hints of hibiscus whisper "Wordsworth!" in tune, where the cats prowl in the rushes of dismay, a barge of twigs and hay and shells plies carelessly its unwieldy wooden sail, creaks out the message of perfunctory freedom and commerce, drawing unerringly with its wavering wake across the faces of George and Grace the frightful distinction of line between freedom which is tartar and slavery which is self. "I had not cried these several years." A tree topples down the slope and is planks on the silver, frothing and sighing. "No more had I." And the crawling diagram falters in the eye of human dispassion and grows less relentless upon the bosom of "The Maiden of the Roses."

George: Fame. How would she know you if you came?

Now the wind has shifted, a breath of snow crumbles across southern Italy towards the pair who, hand in hand, think only of sunsets. The delicate hair of a goat, slipping upon the glassy heights and daintily painting the dizzy rants of green with his carcass, crushes its spangling horns in the sand of the stippled water, spied by a white-spouted steamer on the ocean far. How has our hero wandered?

Grace: Faster and faster pleasure has wounded me. As if its mouth were mine, to be beseeched and not beseeched. I can, at no carmine hour, remember the words the wizard said would save me.

George: Do you remember in far December how the spokes glittered and wheeled and promised? I fainted near the door, knowing I was you, and you disappeared in charge of the currency which had risen, had fallen, on your own sable brow. Could you have meant less, could you have trapped me and forgiven me, could you have relented and freed me? Is that the meaning of these faces in your eyes, the same faces though infinitely varied and hung?

Grace: As once in the dark photograph where the two faces pondered the floor, the one whose chin rested on the part in my scalp, you must know that in our time the crowd has gone home and the presses are silent, finger to lid. I remember only the betrayal within myself which I sought like a seed. Your claim is just, and will become a joke. Why should not my art, which is highest, not rend us both? My will is off the safety and, like a malarial mist, our personal tombstones are wreathed with the iddity of enormous circumstance, which is the substance of life. See that prisoner of Chillon who committed the only crime, the poetic crime.

Now to be busy the streets have come out before dawn and run and run and run, though never celebrating or alternating. All green lights read "wait" and all red read "tell." A crisp hungness of the Morning Star. When to the azure of our several beds we leave "our private walks and arborways, common pleasures, to walk abroad and recreate yourselves."

George: I have thought of those fabulous heroes who sank beneath the heaving torrents of Sardanapalus like a pleasure of furs. Since there is no heaven you may summon all the devils who amuse you across these anguished faces which crouch and beseech. You could conceive the emptiness as clarity, but who listens? who sees? It is as well to stroll on the edge of an abyss like the great Atlantic; uncharted it gave comfort to the last gargantuan sea monsters, and in the clear light of the oceanographer did not fail to sink the Titanic.

In your wandering confidence you will soon find evil imaginary and be proud of the creations of your only too, now, accurate improvisation, thinking of death as existing solely by your power of art; until one day in the forgotten assurance of the heel of the masters you will topple, my poor darling, into a blackness which perceived your insight and fed you and waited and did not weary of your work, like a little girl who amuses her friends with terrifying tales of robbers while Jack the Ripper is picking the lock of the bedroom door.

Grace: Stick by me.

Mercifully the clouds marshal their density and cover the waters as the great public life of our times, which has come out on the slopes of the mountains as it did in "The Miracle of the Loaves and the Fishes," falls sobbing on its earth. Adieu, my twins.

[New York, February 1952]

It's the Blue

The character actor with a rumbling tire
of fat racing his midriff sank deep
in the bath tub and did not scrub
up. There was smoke, bubbles, et cetera.

"Oh how we love punctuation! don't
we?" was what Myers thought voluntarily
when he found the body of that, wow!
particular marionette on its wet back.

He (John Myers) had just roared a
mighty roar having occurred to hisself
primarily some responsibility for certain
ideas: the psychology of the poor, f'raninstance,

or maybe a similitude de Vautrin.
Oh he's nasty, nasty. Nevermind,
Mexico is mad for him, and how! he
goes over there like a pontoon of silk,

the yellow haired revolver of his smile.
At tipsy toast time he fastens his ass
to one of those la-de-da Italian chairs
and screams his commitment to the roast.

But still: John in this emergency's excited.
After all, burly policemen may run in, those
truly blue ones, and hasn't he embarrassed
all those paintings with his smile of a baffled

satyr? It ain't easy to deal with a hero
up to his eyes in the azure of your own bath
and dead as the spirit of Brotherhood. In a fix,
that's John. Maybe the morals of a Waldemar

can help, that man whose circulating ambivalence
seeks always the well lit airport of an epigram.
If not, John's at the mercy of his humiliation
on the bony knees of death. Grant that he remain

so! so glassy an image of our whitest nights
under slipping trees. Yet Waldemar must say
"Poof! you are in love with affairs, messy feeder!
a Navy issue rubber life raft, inflated more

by your desire than gas. The vapors in that salle
rise from your fiendish fiction. What looks up
a corpse is only bruises from your nudging. There's
no physiognomy hitched to that mist. Face

the ceiling zero with a strut in the sky. It's
always right and always wrong and, above all! there.
Jesus, John, get hold of yourself." Poor John
looks tubward and in tears. See, slowly,

the water's getting yellow, sparse hair covers
the walls like a waterfall pouring backwards. Yes,
there's another color starting that I dassn't say.
With the fish hook yawning in his heart John's

flotsam in the heart rending trade winds of now.
Even in this sordid oval, water freezes into mirror
of life. "If this actor isn't dead" cries John
to Waldemar "then I am!" and the ardent insight

of the abandoned paints for him amidst stars
his face and Waldemar's opposed as on a platter.
His role of involvement bars John from the wings
of theory, its static relief of rambling ever;

and if a bubble splits the skin of that tightening
pool he can but scream his despair to hoarse tiles
calling this moment. Any friend would beg him
not to ring the police, but they reach for him

when he's alone to press the buzzer and giggle
as he hands forth his clever wrists. "Divine
absurd!" cries John "I've always embraced you!"
The coppers stamping uniform skies. That's not death.

[New York, February 1952]

Jacob Wresting

For the angel is to be
always at your terrible
shoulder, don't vague out
about trouble in the white
laboratory. Should I frame
my immaculate nose up

in eyelashes and the wives
of great composers you'd find
fustier wreaths resting on
the fat college boys of
middle Michigan anent I laugh
because I'm so muscular.

What misery can be too
rhetorical, as lipstick on
an ass, pretender to a cottage
called "Cineraria" the quite
frumpy and half awash with
elevators always plunging?

Poem

Rat's nest, at home bungling, up
from the wharves into the cradle
and whose arms? be it mine, the pest.
My decision is to say yes, it's
yes always from these brown lips,
sublime monotony and ease of.
To the present trees and to
the crowd hoping to approach
the manhole I cry my magic and
utterly known messages which are
merely remarks. It is enough to know
enough, upper of you cute rats nesting
forever in the warmest armpit. Hand
me my hammer, I go to the toilet.

Down the avenue races the darling
her hair streaming in the wind
crying his handsome name to icicles.
She plunges towards the cold surface
of the river nicknamed "Three Cards"
and the final tinkle is his surname
on her skull. It is enough to know
not what to do. The beasts drink
her blood where it floats on ice,
but they all come back to nest and
even the neighbors know how I smell
in the springtime. It's a habit
acquired in youth, nice to animals.

[New York, March 1952]

A Darkened Palette

The rooftops are all cluttered up,
an old cat lies out in the rain sop
        belly-up, and the rouge cheeks
        between her outstretched arms, the bricks

between snaky chimney pots
and chunks of soot like clouds, slates
        with holes for hanging niggers,
        are limp and slippery. The figures

would blossom tumbling tots, sliding
beaming and fast riding
        the ropes of our eyes if night
        only filled the bowls of our sight

with its rumbling tulips of
coffee. I cannot light above—
        oh Nellie take the kettle
        off, pour ink upon the cattle

and beware the lamp that
would finger night's melting heat
        upon the empty paper sky,
        its itchy purple belly.

The cat is going up in smoke,
quite young, and singing in the black
        with shiny claws to trace
        the leafy trees, its choice.

[New York, April 1952]

Poem

"It's only me knocking on the door
of your heart" whined the radio
while I bawled feverishly, eating
an orange, salting it up a little.

A gelatin light squeezed windows
I had watched all night at, bored,
lordy was I bored. I thought maybe
some bombers would fly over or

something. No, I was really nuts,
miserable. I called Jane and John
and Al and Waldemar and Grace and then
got scared, hung up, screamed!

and couldn't get out a window
because I'd locked them all, because
I'm six flights up. And it's been a
terribly cold winter, radio's been broke.

[New York, April 1952]

67

The Beach in April

"Not to be palatial like a Spanish busboy
and not to be scrumptious, that's not you"
Jane said, frowning and left hand pounded
sand under my eyes, fine free spinning

knifing the space between sea and horizon,
spine I was to fill with Mercedes Benz ears.
Narcissi spilt to the crest of all waves as
her nylon ruffles spat from under her skirt

blowing forth like flags. My eyes worked quietly
at their pearls. The international amity
of that froth above her knees travelled nowhere
like a music, the stinging black transportation

of suns. The perfect pressure of our hearts,
no escapes into the sky and no bitterness of coins,
a leaf and a trumpet against the belted parkway
of changing roadsters rampant in lipstick maroon.

"From this day we have never left all others
behind us, caught a familiar face, me, Jane,
trapped in the bamboo." Our freezing feet. Only
that shaggy upright practicing as the blue falls.

A Wind at Night

The blonde murdered
in the moonlit woods
    in the eye's cool water
    escapes each sigh

of the superficially
gentle and tangential
    surface dalliance,
    so sweetly throttled!

her soft nipples nest
where the birds' young curl
    in their round jewels,
    in polished unpleasantness.

Her cry is our silence
against the motionless blood
    against the pumping brain
    and an expanse of science,

she sings out sweet life
in a wake of sandy spittle,
    as our dreams burst feebly
    out of her cracked eyes.

[New York, May 1952]

69

Prose for the Times

Yesterday I accepted an invitation to a party. But I had no sooner arrived and let my coat tumble, exhausted, onto a bed, when a perfect stranger whom I immediately and unwittingly admired asked me if I were a poet.

Many guests crowded around the two of us, as at a wedding. "I suppose I am," I said, "for I do write poems."

"Well write one now, will you?" he said, smiling fiercely, faces aureoled at his shoulders and elbows. A few tendrils of hair escaped the opening of his shirt, fled upward to his neck, and they were not the color of his eyebrows!

"I'm sorry, but I don't feel like one just now, if you don't mind," I said, thinking of many things, chiefly, perhaps, of childhood, when I would make myself vomit so I wouldn't have to go to parties.

"Well, what makes you feel like writing one?" he said, and kicked me in the balls.

Ugh!

As I hobbled to a chair, however, I managed to somewhat regain my composure. "You needn't be afraid of me," I said, turning. "I don't love you."

[New York, May 1952]

[Tent-digging on the Vacant Lakes We Appled]

Tent-digging on the vacant lakes we appled
lame, and whistling a revelry of levers.
The puritans were fond of sun and loon
but they ate parts of noon-ripened horses,
buffed their livers and suppered the solitude,
resting in sieves their marvelous coffee.
I'm talking about dreams' derailed ouiji,
I love the cracked tooth of an old aunt,
I melt when an orange weeps its grenadine
and raises aloft a sweetmeat under the marquee.

[Southampton, May 1952]

Maurice Ravel

That in the living, the fastening
seashells onto skyscrapers, syncopating
the lozenges, oh beauty! indestructible
you have become by his hands.

The harmful distances of silence
somewhat abated, he can finally rest
in your brain companioned by tempestuous
thoughts, walking him up and down,

waltzing him round, always with
love and discrimination self-taught.
Removing the silencer from the gun
he shot agates into your eyes, fell

upon the weak cries of infants
with leonine roars from backyard fences
and did not falter before the bolero's
dumb desert. His wrist dripped oases.

If, at the untellable hour of quiet,
he had not put fingernail to
waterglass, what trees we'd've
turned to! fugitive, quivering.

[New York, May 1952]

72

"Red"

Red ringlets in the sunset!
what buttery nostalgias you joke,
what pianistic sallies into the past!
up to my ears in elephants!

Oh landscape dewy with sequins,
we're not artificial are we?
And when winter comes, we won't
go inside and drink watered rum?

The hunters are acting like sharks
and the whores like laburnums,
gourmets finger toothpicks
and diplomatists fight cholera,

throughout the world of Free Men
a supple voice is ringing "Join";
and yet your dyed hair disappears
against these swooning and tiered waves,

whom I was never asked to come meet
but got to know the way of the bulb
when its surprising smugness trips
over springtime, although it's merely colors.

That upcoming acid's already eating
into the rippling vermilion situation,
but I will contain you this moment
which is not so cheap as blood.

[New York, June 1952]

73

Serenade

This night this forest
which purple arrest

clutches the moon,
the noisy baboon

of her screams
as loon she streams

her lacerations
through the stations

of treetops' flown
flowers and thin down

towards the ceiling
of the sea's healing

thunder. O loves
enamored of doves

and other bloody
tenderness of body!

shabby in the eyes
of sleeping flies

your sand hovers
and lights movers:

as in your lies
the sun dies.

[New York, June 1952]

A Sunday Supplement

The 'scape turns bloody,
clouds pant,
    steam rises,
        a rainbow raises
its Tea Pot Dome over the years

since you and I were
young,
    Maggie, Sally,
        Bill and Betty,
Elsa, Andy, Burton and Carolyn.

The alabaster columns
in the bushes,
    all broke to hell,
        don't recognize
the kids, we've gone over the hill!

Then we never missed
the funnies,
    didn't know then
        the dopy soldier
and flighty Waac would leave us colder

than sweet Debussy,
Max Nordau
    anonymous dancers
        and Maggie Teyte,
or boyish Bill with's Herbert Spencer.

We loved our bodies,
navyblue sneakers,
    Frank Sinatra
        and pistachio frappes,
it's all in our heart and dirtied there

without a bath of
tears or war,
    with the help of
        the Zeit and of the
Geist on the western divan in the bare

cupboard where
adolescents plot;
    never have so many
        been so happy with so
little. We loved the bright first pot.

[New York, June 1952]

Kra Kra

The nut cracks come
when I'm chatting dumb

to some dumbbell on
the shore who every dawn

brings them me, as if
I never got a whiff

of a nut by myself.
I like it by myself.

How could I get such
a sharp tongue and soft touch!

if I didn't hunt better
than an Irish setter

for at least native nuts
and the rain-mild butts

that slipped from under
mustaches in afternoon thunder

or at the theater.
I'm no great eater,

though now it's fun
to amuse someone and one

is amused, I guess.
But it's embarrassingly less.

The sea seems deeper.
The sky seems steeper.

Learned the belly roll
since moon I was stole

from the frigate *Yes Marie.*
Not lonesome, no sirree.

Miss those ocean voyages
to Carthage and Troy, ages

of cursing bearded men.
You locked up my hen.

[New York?, 1952]

A Protestant Saint

about Dick Mayes

And the day's that are dead
like rusty sewing machines,
silent and on the fritz,
still jangle in his left ear.
He thinks holds his lover's
voice by telephone through strife
and hurricano. Well there's no
tell and no gale, the night
is moony. A woman in bedclothes
knocks at the door and cries
"Your open window's flooding
my sash, the plaster's turning
brown and dripping!" but
it's really his mother, a way
of punishing him for pissing
on that tea rose. The window rests
upon the city's velvet cushion.
He lies on a green couch, writhing
says that he has fantasies God
he down a woman's underwear of stairs
approaches. Is smiling as he comes.

[New York, June 1952]

What Sledgehammer? or
W.C. Williams's Been Attacked!

Yester the heat I walked my tiglon "Charles F"
around the Park, as three nuns in a stationwagon
(au Zoo) robbed the Elizabeth Arden Building.
In the University pistols were not shot off

because they aren't "clean precise expression." Ho
ho ho, kra, chuh, chuh, tssk tssk tssk, tereu. They
stole barrels of rice powder (yeastfully ruched), white
like angels' balls, the ever-chucked and careless Fs.

And there's going to be a wedding! there's going to be a
We-Know-What-To-Do-In-The-Fall (a Ball!) between
the Metatheosophists with Italian bedbugs
swinging from their woolly nipples and *The Hudson Review*

(that Organ). And nobuddy invites, except Boola-boola:
the crowd that paints "Elegance a Thoroughfare
to Yellow Drawers, the Commonwealth of Closed Cavities"
on the Town (get it?) Line. Indian afternoon, my dirty.

[New York, June 1952]

Latinus

Ancestral is as doves, some
    invisibly paw an Egyptian mantle
like chargers. An old rathead
    myself alone and a promising daughter,

the laurels fall all over her
    when she walks unbundled groveward.
And that day she burst in flames,
    her charred tiara in the rattled streets,

I wept premonitive amidst spades
    and leaves: Fear the raving prow
which cleaves its grave historically
    towards your darling's shore! Now how

I, old fatheart, kissed Albunean dung
    before prophetic Faunus and the giggling
of fountains, which are orators. The great
    are gone. Turned to swine-snouts at the root.

[New York, July 1952]

The War

The war pleased me to know of my interest
and came and went like fog. The garden, wandered
of my true delight delectable, had changed her face
and where the gate had stood horrible teeth
opened on tribal hinges to outcast me. Yet
had I become gone for something rare, and dreaded
no punishment so much as its betrayal in flesh
I saw identical. To push always onward!
over the hill, to other homes that might be laid
in ruin, beautiful sunset of the fist! sole
amusement for the renegade who wears the colors
of some brushed-by conquistador. "A mean one"
the cops say, they can always tell us, not that there
are many. And it is so. Black souls inside black eyes.
No mirrored world. You part the curtain;
the muzzle stares into heaven of its own choosing
and recoils at the competitive vulgarity of targets.
I'm back and you and you drop plates, seeing the puffs
of dust spring from a door that's dead to my white clenches.

[July 1952]

The Builders

Green pyjamas renting themselves out
on the boardwalk of a foreign city. I'm
not undone, but they're gassing about me
at Brighton. In the midst of plenty I found

my meal and couldn't sit for the sunburn.
How many twinges make a recoil? I walk
the planks searching for splinters. There,
no place a man can be a man in piece.

If construction mattered then wickedness
would falter and virtue rise assured
like a dental appointment. That moment won't,
for the flowers. It simply does not occur.

You are right to feature the tan entertainer
at an ebony piano beneath a driftwood lamp
on the fringe of the success of an older spoon.
"It aint me, it aint me, it aint me, dig dig dig."

[East Hampton, July 1952]

[With the Minute Intentions
of a Boa Heroic Constrictor]

With the minute intentions of a boa heroic constrictor
　　　he rescued the maid
who wore trousers in the dun berried solarium
　　　and had fiddled
away a fortune in platinum kangaroo pouches
　　　to be blown up
like photographs in the crockery mouth of the tropics.
　　　He had wanted
a detachment from the archdiocese to plant crops
　　　and plan publicity
but they sent a carload of damson crumbling to dust
　　　against the pond.
"Think in the natural mug these coughing precautions!"
　　　sobbed Maidie,
"and a mother worth of attentions stinging my ears!"
　　　warned her away.
So in pink pyjamas she bedded the three producers,
　　　her Jap uncles.

[East Hampton, July 1952]

Changing Your Ways

I recently met this rav who's a relative
of Rabbi Bou who looks Assyrian.
I'd recently renounced my religion.

I was still in the mood so enamored
how this rav could try his soul
like an elevator button, that sweaty

and that sure of which heights. "I'm
not the most ambitious of living, dear
Frank, to chide you for loving me."

[East Hampton, July 1952]

Study of Women on the Beach 2

"When his hand reaches me I imagine
the very stars are sisters." She turns
as if someone were throwing a medicine.

"My day was scandalous! it burns
and straggles. He did it me in Oshkosh.
It was one of those transcontinental firsts.

I shrieked with delight. He squash
winner and marathon fantastic swore
the wallpaper rippled. They said lush

but'e was generous to the fault of the future."
Animated and in drapes dropped dead,
the dear man who had watered her flower away.

85

Poem
"Le Paradis n'est pas artificiel"

The rich cubicle's enclosure
with its verdant pasturage and fences
        to keep the pussyfoots out
and its leagues of seaboard tentacles
        of azure dripping down stalactites
or perhaps the simple sea of memory's dove
staying forever in the walled air which coos
        sadly and (as it were) rancidly

Because all of that had failed to find him. The
Times had suddenly gone into a nose dive
(from swearing on Elsa too often and too much?)
Don't look so much Wagner said when asked
if the Alps were really strategically impossible
what other kind of canto is there? the voice
of Kurt Schwitters purling like nightingale stubs
over the urinating cellicule and over ripe riven Pisa
the trepidating torts thereof
                Render unto Ez
the things that are Ezra's. and unto God
the things that are not ours. When the pupil
of the day came templar and cried "I must be
about my pater's business" you did not quiz him
        if he be democratical or not.
those professors are not more nor less precise
than us cowboys us bung-hole blowers of
        Venice-on-Hudson Atlantic New York.

                [New York, August 1952]

August Afternoon, a Collage

"She's no Bohemian, you understand, but she does
the mostly irresponsible things. I think she's nuts.
The guanaco's nose is soft like one of your grey French
and let's go. Fllllpppw! Well they should be. You might
as well come over here in public and take a bath, Boom-boom
ain't over there. Oh let him have a little suck. Nanna!"
PLEASE DO NOT FEED BIRDS ON LAWN "I think Marty's
lost. Here, birdie. You know they bite once in a while?
Just wait till he gets a little popcorn, god, is it terrible.
Well, he can study to be a doctor as well as the next.
Yeahahahaha. He hasn't been well and then his wife Thelma
broke her hip. Uh, where do you go in the country? I don't
want to have to hold this kind of pail, it drops." FREE
WATER FOR HORSES

                      "Then pass me gently into this silence
of mashers and rollerskates where the red-white-and-blue
so coolly flips, the hotel where Waldemar hacked, penthouse,
watched the primary lozenges of traffic, met me at the Automat
for lunch." GO THE MOTOR COACH WAY "It's the envy of Boston!"

                                    [New York, August 1952]

[The Azure Waves Grumble and Languish]

CHIA: The azure waves grumble and languish
upon the shoulders of California,
the fleecy sloops plunge in sinking suns
and the birds drown with them gallantly,
like old-fashioned soldiers. Weep
here where the Pacific's flat distends
in the eye ball, glazing the ghosts
of our sons, poor yellow Americans,
so that we seem to see them, see.

SSU: Ahi, ahi. It is murderous, winds
pitching snow at our backs and we
so old, having come down the other
side of the mountain to be greeted
only by the rampant sea. No glade,
no homes, no harbor, and nothing
yet said, just the drear expanse of
mortal heaving and yawning. Dear friend,
whose gnarled company's my total,
don't you fear its rough contemplation?

[New York, August 1952]

[Fish Smells in the Hallway]

Fish smells in the hallway
because it is Friday and cheap,
drifts down the bannisters.
And there's spinach in my bathtub
left from last night. The rye
I just bought will scream when
the top comes off, making
two people ugly, but I must
get to the dinner. To work
tomorrow will be amusing, all
witless faces on their Saturdays.

[New York, October 1952]

Poem About Jane

"You have no idea! you can't know how she has
provoked me while you were away!" he cries! but
"Uh huh, you apparently have forgotten how I
love her" I mutter as I stab him.

[New York, October 1952]

[Rooftops Blocks Away from Me]

Rooftops blocks away from me
laborers push at hods
I am dashed on rocks at sea
they think on of bawds

The careless sun removes itself
night imitates this ease
my painful eyes were made in Delft
and cannot see the trees

Night the wind is tossing cities
I am walking always fear
strangers' lubricated pities
fail to ease me here

Now the darkness drips and fails
the siren's call and dove
awakens the clambering entrails
the labyrinthine love

[1952]

A Birthday

Jane is floating into the Hudson
one breast in the air. A vision
of mountain goats and Vermeer
in a fruit bowl at her flank.

Brushes of azure scud across
her towering white forehead and
the wake of her silver barque
coughs up a billion rumors!

In this gallery of nocturnals
and muscles the planets waltz
to see her lurid dreams repair
to the Eden of our revolving eyes.

[New York?, 1952]

[Of All Community of Mind and Heart]

Of all community of mind and heart
singling out for each its terrible burden
I proffer these and the love which fills it
as fresh water surrounds cut flowers.

In interims and in vales and in torrents
the flesh of these holds its harmonica
to the wind and is ambitious to risk
some terrible sob from the eye of the phalanx,

aristocrats among fiends and prostitutes
before the intellectuals, waiting till snow
falls, and only then hiding. Remember
this fountain when the ocean covers[?] our looks.

A Wreath for John Wheelwright

1

"Yes, these shadows, lengthening into the mind,"
he scrubbed the grey and yellow hedge with wire eraser,
"are at once the line of total vulgarity and of
total intelligibility, taking nicks out of me and you,
yes, they are the razors as must sharpen the temper
of our times, so does my heart to birds at evening
on this withering grass cover each dainty carcass
with a carmine shed. The rarest musicians are today
the flightiest, push me never, hurry me not." Leonardo,
looking onto the lawn from imaginary clouds, although
it was gloomy, let fall some rain and many faces.

2

Just as the moment precludes
the vanishing army and its race
for the toga to wash it, so
the parallel structure of the eyes
must cluster like a snowberry
or crash head on into its own
clarity with all its might. Do
you fence the plains at fourteen
and not remember your dad, Wild
Wendell, the Redskins' fear and joy,
the Brahmins' sufferance? He,
crossing the Rubicon, laid
railroad ties, later suggested
to Tarquin that Lucretia might be
it. Do you remember who got away?
how they all got back to home base
and the flags flew and the newspapers
boomed for weeks? A strikebreaker.

3

Thus rejection had powdered its sister Portugal as a thing
of climate, flimsy frigate will and charmeuse, willful
in that its horse wore sequins, mounting chalky combers
of the sea our poet's forehead luckily sinks in
as the hoof's about to strike. Gutty rolling telephone
of his caprice'll find its Vatican, bequeath a saltcellar
as in the golden days of remorse, schooled to the world
of soup serenaders and poetic predicaments and scourge.

4

Now Wheelwright in a bear coat that wouldn't house
the small forest he had the key to, felt the Old Masters
"So shy and ambling all, and not kicking enough
against the pricks. That classicism had no hammers, no
fat to cook the workers' hands in, no rod for the wasters.

As I go up like a lily, they'll come down like lightning,"
but the critics all thought he'd besmirch his vocables
in the futuristic flatness of the nasal earth which, a bowl
of dust, seemed to ruminate ironically. "Ascension" they
hawed, "is for virgins uneasy at our green cultural sociables,

not for the rancid potpourri which is statues of gardens,
vended to suburbia by helicopter at a commission."
Yet, "Ave!" cried the poet, tearing his junk-hung breast
to the mist and its embracing rust, the dawn that smelled
like an orangery. Those faces were medals, chained permission

on the fierce twin glare of his swan-muscled throat. He,
paranoid and panting, threw his father onto the mat
with a back-blinding jujitsu exclamation. Stepped in the river
and, as the water of voices cooled his ankles, got migraine.
A racing car exploded in the clouds. "God? Could it be that?"

5

Lastly, he strode into Lodestone Gulch, panther
conscious, and star-striving in spurs. This
was most westest of all on the red map
and he the fountainous fortune of which'd been cut
down, the myth of the recaptured. Black cacti
sped their strict screeches onto loading platforms
and burning stanchions of well-chewed miles,
bitten into by all that the West means: the Magi!
the Klondike! And it was a black cat sure enough
that spread its gory kiss between the fingers he
would later turn his head from, drop his agates,
and never so much as pause to deny while shooting
deep that sandy snarling maw whose dumb eyes
splintered the future into clustered breakers of
insight and iron, panic aforesight crusted
as the lava of Barbizons poured in one ear and out
both blinkers. To him. No suffragette pushing wagons
of tedium vitae, "the acquiescent cola," thither
could polish that muddy decade the ranges of flora,
twinkling and dreaming, he'd already pictured himself
Rocky Mountain eagle of. Dew fell from his rising lids
like bullets. As in the identical bed of Sardanapalus,
eastern women flopped and shed; that bloody sail, later
by death and poetry, set panting gill on the Atlantic shore.

[See the Tents and the Tanks and the Trees of March!]

See the tents and the tanks and the trees of March!
The wind screams forth as if everything were stone.
In the middle of the fields I was composed of fire
but I have become more and more mountainous, O my soul.

Intermezzo

I
The cloud is jumping, umbrella of azure, yes,
to awaken counting in a heart asleep.
They are practicing their prairie-sententiousness
up at the villa, with five fingers, irreparable.
And their felicity is più. O world!
Windows of toast flutter through a silence
which is the mystery of melting things.
Reinflamed at the first breast he saw the flock
hoisting its tailfeathers over a grey pond,
a cloudy languor fanned his heart into the air.
Unlike the others, he was smiling, his lips
spattered with snow, whispering "We shouldn't"
while the various banners of intimacy
drifted towards the open sea, reoriented, leaping.
The heavens forced its breath into his ear,
that shell whose echo had already demanded itself
from the music of his furious cut hands.
The glasses sounded like a rainbow at his stroking
from his vinegar-moistened fingers, his tongues.
The taught child always pays attention, dark,
to the morning ices, their distracted peculiar fruits
as they cry out to be wrapped in aluminum foil,
and the savage one stands beside him asking for him
as if to be younger were to be a priest.
That particular map they found, we found, for them,
is for ridiculous travels that tire you out
for you must know the pure water of a mask;
cannot doubt be surrounded like a roulette wheel
and sexual performances be applauded by children?
The elegants do stroll in dinner clothes

down the immense valley of fir trees and oranges
where smoke rises protectingly against the hail.
You wish to be heard above the massed forgetfulness
of a full orchestra against a drop of the Virgin Mary
painted in chiffon? Let's call it "Everything"
for swan, saxophone, child and orchestra, arranged
for four hands by the composer who didn't invent the cup.
You see me very clearly, don't you, here on the floor
of the world looking for my recording apparatus.
They have just risen without a sought clacking
but I will not shoot a bird in flight, no matter
that my navel is on the return trip from my spine.
The air, the air, the air, the never air!

II
If you see a rose fall into the sea
study its selfish repining after hares
in the grinding fjords of night.
This target is sewn with pearls.
You will find a black glove of birds
in the crotch of the Ambassador to Negligence.
It forms an invisible tissue with the epaulet
one mile to the right, and all who run this path
snap their necks. Only kangaroos escape.
There is a piano beside the desk of myrtle.
The Seven Ages of Freedom are lining up for the race.
I am oinking into a distance that cannot displease you.
Wind, be with me! Oh rapture of four cloven legs,
oh twinklers in the Milky Way of my mouth!
whose gums are roseate with English toothpaste and blood.

III

How many days have you been gone, oh athletes
of color? Between my brass shoulders you have laid
me bare, you have separated my thorns and entered
the brilliantly bubbling grotto of shade.

Where the passage of night has thundered
and gone unopened you have stretched and leaped
with burning silver grins that moved you up.
Didn't you know I was poison, to be cut and heaped?

He strode to the center of the lights and cried
"I was brought up on having my knife taken away
by them, so I am unhurt but unhappy. Won't someone
drown me in rainbow trout, and masturbate and pray

for me until I am entirely gone into flowers?
Oh great bed of the world, don't I deserve you?
your great hands closing over my thighs
in the slender kiss of your unweeping blue?

I have resisted the rosy temptations
and their pastured snares and religions' high
fragility. I have earned nothing. I have not been
picturesque. Take me, as if I were wounded, into the sky."

[New York, January 1953]

[My Country,
Leafy and Blue with Infinite Breaths,]

My country, leafy and blue with infinite breaths,
somehow I shall escape into history, the valor of a heart
shall not refuse that punishment, I would burn
all characteristics, all intimacies, from a forehead
already too lofty; scoop out the golden plains, not
to feed the multitudes but to create vast sea beds
of the future, into which all mountains eventually must
relinquish their monuments, their thoughts of air.
Then, facing total blackness, I am at last my self.

[New York, February 1953]

Clouds

How will I be able to keep you
if you don't disgust me a little?
Why do you wear lipstick with trousers
that are stained and stain?

At the end of the raspberry patch
I found my own darling telephone
hiding away like a little reservist.
Why do you disgust me?

I can't see the bridge any more.
"You look like a Dutch interior."
"Then I guess I do know how pretty I am."
But it is not dark, it is very sunny.

I wish that you would await me
without your horse near the windbells
on the path to the left of the jonquils.
If you just jangle your spurs I'll know,

but who else would it be, anyway?
and if something tinkles it'll be
one of your threaded silver bracelets
that you cover with your cuff before cops.

I want you to stop making me sick.
I want you to go away and not stay away.
Could you bring me razor blades when you come back?
and a sandwich of begonias and glass?

[New York, February 1953]

Causerie de Gaspé Peninsula

"You're not really brown." "Sometimes I think
I have too many breasts. The king and his knights
went to the church under a ravishing mantle
of blue all stitched with air currents. Mary Magdalene!
the boats were foundering in the banks." "I put down
the towel and suddenly a hideous stain appeared
on the open pages of the book, it was *Inclinations*
by England's famed Ronald Firbank and I read the legend
'Your name is mud.' Now how do you like that?"
"I'll buy that as sure as my tie is a livid welter
of smeared smut. Heavens! what am I doing wearing a towel?
You seem to be bursting into song. Are you?"

"When mere illness to the one side is wasted,
clang around as if emptying a farewell,
don't send alimony to the leaf forever rising
and don't play Tug-of-War with the deer.

When an ache is going bald in the dumps
be the most beautiful stimulant ever spilled on a floor
of a saloon in the mountains of Lightness, Tennessee.
Are you nearer to the jute, or are you on a jag?
I hate to think of you dragging yourself around
because the seriousness of a ring lies in the hand.
Do you seem to be farting? Always the adventurer!
I stutter, but I am behind you and I am still standing.
The dock is going sideways into a feathery lust,
and the lift is become balsam, like a tuba in a wagon."

"What a lovely idea! If I race you to Beddoes Island
backwards will you really caress me on Easter as you say?
I already feel like an egg!" "No. I hate you." "Liar!"

[New York, February 1953]

St. Simeon

Welcher, and leg of the world,
does sin beg a habit from us?
The least nit of a forsaking
wonders how to cry, and we
are brightened by a rumor of him
dashing into the fray well lighted.
Amidst sightseeing strangulations
we are fables, straddlers of joy,
seated in the mild Altogether
of a cage. And it is a mountain.
Weird and living, repeatedly
the rushes open in our soul
in motioning its sky-traveller
hitherward and starry, bleeding
perhaps and hairy of buttock;
it is a bold blue stare
itching its way into the dark
of the lonely poet on his stick
in the heights of a posture
which is opposed to sainthood.

And has the voice of that flag
ever failed us? like brimstone,
the sheer ineffectuality of it
glancing into the white sky
has been a powerful curse of joy.

[New York, March 1953]

Light Cavalry

O toe! o kiss on the sleeping back of my head!

two women sleeping on each other's shoulders, bent
like a marble arbor over the breasts of the dead.
A wind, magnificent in their extremity, cloaks us in spent

pleasures, and in fossilized tresses "the last
of England." What a blue look the couch is separating!
and where I peer into your white smile a mast
is borne into the summer air, the sparrows! striating

roars in a heart trembling with nostalgias
and their sweaters of foresight and funicular
pain-is-a-fir-tree. While the milk of Manhattan's algae
grazes its own slopes we shore in love that's tubular,

humming "Sous les toits de Paris" in colored nightmares
which are exhilarating to look saltily back at. Night!
isn't that why you're known as "the Hardtack"? these airs
that seem such a stanch support and are merely Delight

hanging up its woodbine? The regatta closes in
suddenly, and a tuning fork smeared with blood cries
balefully, its languid arms wrapped around the mizzen,
and the upper sails dip lustless as barrages to eyes

that are taxis, nay perambulators! So it is dirt, the
glamorous grey of it upon the lip. The hill, the hill,
the hill, the hill! If white dancing to bare the lies, see,
to him, he suddenly won't loathe me any more, the skill

of being any place else, dead, but I'd love to be you
and sick, and any time your black eyes' rocks' flares
incarcerate me I'll be resting only then, being blue,
the osteopath! he's terrifying, and when he stares

into your knees they just close up like mountains
of seas, "I'm-a-little-drunk-dear-phone-calls," mountainous
ease is what I mean of the medical profession. "Own towns"
they will tell you, but it's hormones make you fountainous,

not manipulation. How can I the miraculous scenery
of my life dissuade? It's the opposite of Sisyphus, and
will replace my nape, that buttered seat of venery,
with the prairied shoulders of a friendly hand:

"Who wages war with a dark brown gift, a war"
surely knows the weight of his love. Grand Opera.

[New York, March 1953]

Addict-Love

A Jew.
His jowls, particolored, semi-precious stubble.
A Jew, an Arachne, his anxiety quells and tramps his
      moaning navel, his Marchy loins.
The average out-of-sortness and cupidity climbs fault-
      lessly, pouring out rhinestones, rhinestones from
      the Rhine,
and I latch onto that which utterly paralyzes my un-
      decipherable prepuce.
I get trench mouth, jouncing in convertibles, romp-
      ing without rubbers, ferrying myself grinning
      jailers.
At a clip that's disgusting to the martyrs in my set,
      I combine with limpidly smelly daisy chains my
      magnificently amiable pairs of achingly defiled
      "friends,"
void myself like someone punching oboes, who's bovine
      enough to move in musical tights,
occupied with riddles, with Chicagoans (after all,
      what's the sense of missing a mischance?), with
      claquing singers who've sloughed off their voices
      in an effort to grow fatter; Jews pulsate through
      my framework like a crayon left on the swooning
      tombstone that's like a sarong under one of those
      palm trees sucking low and long over the lagoon
      at midnight neath the lip of the moon, see it
      sluggish, see it slapdash, see it slumbrous, as
      it will die,
rot, tooth to one cacophonously humiliated in the tropics
      where the tailed ones swim, oh niggling parachute
      of spring milk in truffled dugs!

cramming the desk drawer of each touchy ministration
        with my real rancor, this fainting rancor which
        quails before the ideological nervy-but-nice
        dynamite
nudging quauhaugs of harems, and estaminets.
Put your lips against the end of the line (or "meat-
        puss"), send me, send de gum drops.

Nerveux, absentees, share-croppers of the liver-lip,
        dump your Uncle Dan, the gringo, unlessen yourself
        of the whole counter-light-bulb movement that's
        fading into importance,
I'm explaining it to you.
Smell, smile, a year away, and let fly your jumping
        corneas of mon-ami-miracle-mix too openly in-
        cautious to be calculated to blush
and then force the nipple,
and bite …
and stare …

[New York, March 1953]

[En Route to the Burial in Long Island]

En route to the burial in Long Island
two sullen lower East Side thugs—
well known to the safe and loft squad—
received prizes and reigned at a Hawaiian feast
at Bayville, once it's put on the face.
A giant screen with stereophonic sound,
the double-barrelled, triple-powered,
forty-five calibre rocker socker of the year,
encouraged Rhee to carry on his desperado activities.

[Southampton, April 1953]

Perfumes

1

Sentimentality! aren't you sunset?
isn't the warrior with coal black eyes
in his arms carrying a Union suit
over his shoulder and thinking of spies?
I had luncheon with Grace today and then
dined with Elaine on Armenian rice
but late drinks were dumped down with Red Helen.
For, you see, having appointments is nice.
And isn't it distressing to see them
all in one day as if one didn't know
who one's friends were? like a picture of Shem?
I didn't think that I wanted to go
      but I went for a swim in the sunset.
      Beautiful women! are you in Onset?

2

And there's the necessity for being
an African sculpture. And the dark sand
of garrulous love, which is like seeing
oneself in a three-dimensional hand
on a screen amidst the cheering children.
Because you were never under a bed
has your enthusiasm been killed, then?
Helen thinks everything she's slowly said
is an ocean-chart by Marie Mencken,
sandy and luminous at night, but plans
like these are only as useful to men
as their imaginations in sampans
      steaming up and down the Yellow River
      of the heart, its own eternal giver.

3

Ah, my own nervous Grace, how strong she is!
willing to be terrible all the time
but never quite making it. What is this?
at the very moment of her sublime
force she's already capitulating
to the graciousness of her blonde white taste
which she'd been writing letters to, hating.
And it's no wonder that she leaves in haste,
knowing that her beauty's nothing to her
just as the wet grass doesn't help the ground,
and Nothing's interested in the sewer;
Nothing's said to like Theater-in-the-Round.
  No, she has never really gone away.
  She's intimate, and long as a good day.

[Southampton, April 1953]

[Lace at Your Breast]

Lace at your breast
can be pulled and eaten

into the foam of your lips
I plunge like a hare

flaunting the pole of sunlight
you careen undercurrent

my Victoria of salmon falling
my bushel of trees and

launching your supreme smile
the sea is no vast fear

109

Joseph

Oh my suppurating ears!
there is too much wind in the flushed canyons.
Across the hills another's
cloak surveys the loathsome dispassionate millions.

I am red before the bar
and stare like an evil son of Judeah whose purpose
is what the songs are;
oh Max Jacob, where is your adipose?

tonight, who are you blind?
Let me escape to my enormous tent in a trance,
let me faint across the wind.
I have discovered soldiers doubting at the entrance,

it is what I've always feared.
From now on I shall refuse to walk ahead of anybody.
When I was very free, seared
of myself, and set out to contaminate worlds, my body

gave pleasure that was not
mine to become famous for, not yet a disgusting air,
nor ambiguous in fault.
I am a prophet still, and you are a host in this affair.

[New York, May 1953]

110

Spleen

JACK::   A ramp of muscle runs from my chest to my groin
        and on this magnificent catwalk the crabs
        invite their friends the fleas to a big meal
        of coconut fiber and gas. O golden earth
        of my bony shoulders, must we always fall upwards!
        isn't it wonderful to be alive? aren't they glad?
        And when I exert myself the tendons stand out,
        rigid as neon, grinning tightly as they struggle.
        It's amusing to see the sun wither so many germs
        after you've been asleep, really preoccupied
        with hell. I love to think of their delicacy
        as they flutter along my stomach and their avarice
        in jousting the feathery vermin of my nature's
        affectionate stance, those dear ones who are selfish
        and truly proprietary, who only feed on what you are.
        But it is too much trouble to be discriminating,
        isn't it? And we shouldn't care, we're so reflective.
        But don't you wonder how the sky will look
        when the clouds are entirely brushed away by the cruelty
        called "azure," and a heady wind is lending its ear
        to your real desires? the sententiousness, the pats-
        on-the-ass, the emptiness that's like a dirigible
        filled with old skin, the amusingly classical pain.

ANNE: The mothers go on asking you to reject their sons,
        the lissome infatuated men. They don't know what pride is.

[New York, May 1953]

Forest Divers

Fellow-trees, bell so frail and brown
outroaring charm, paces,

aren't you dreaming of ruby watches?

Do you feel in your voice-box
and in its salt response
quite humble and arbitrary?
and is it a ticket to Rangoon
and are you rusty like a fox?

Elbow lifted to plunge and rend,
elephant of the Nilus waters,
elucidate always the choice of propriety,
elegantly trailing eyes.

[Southampton, May 1953]

The Weekend

Who are you looking for, pink book?
All the locomotive engineers have rose fever
and Long Island, the Siberia of the tourist,
is sounding like Old Faithful in a bus.
Tonight we improvised a conversation
between two drunkards with lisps and afterwards
made jello but it had pineapple in it.
The trains hate pineapple, it just won't burn.
In London I read your Naples diary, in Frisco
I didn't have time to read, how are you?

The snow was whirling like a picture frame
but I bought the tie anyway and gave it to the
snarling helicopter, but it passed me by.
O lavender kitchen equipment, aren't you
the seriousness that passed me by? the cloud
of tools clanging, that will keep coming back
like Old Faithful in a bus? who asked you anyway?
It's too late to become a priestly transvestite
because all the shops are closed and the candles
are hid. And who wants to monkey around with monkeys?

The Lights over the Door

1
O fountains of Christopher Street!
it is autumn and the fleas,
have you evaded the Shore Patrol and got into "Mary's"?

2
Where the leaves were catapulting down
one flea took out her Rosary
and began to intone in falsetto and very near

3
"O Holy Mother Church, you are the green
vestment on the back stoop
where the prisoners are flipping like cradled fish."

4
Then there was a dark cloud and the prisoners,
they ceased to be amused
by the charity circus that had gotten into their vest,

5
for they were very religious
as poisoners go and go off,
and were all dressed like lion tamers to the hilt

6
and to the hilt Christopher Street.
O the ghastly tear bombs!
they were ravishingly handsome in their nuns' habits,

7
which they had rented from a sexton
who was an ex-disk jockey.
You may well have sat down and gawked at their youngness,

8

you pompous idiot, "very mysterious"
when they are all getting shot
by a bunch of well-armed fleas with the red eyes

9

of a movie magazine, twenty-five.
Did you disrobe before animals?
Yes, father, but that was after I was arrested. Hey!

10

the tulips are absolutely crawling
like young girls who know men.
Aren't you ordering the innumerable hearses yet to come?

11

You must not be brazen with me,
my darling, I know you fell down
inside the ice-cream cone and like to drown yourself

12

when the lights go out. Orange taxis!
and the absence of breath odor.
It is impersonal to be next in line in history,

13

feeling the oats you stole
from the horse, his blue teeth
over which the hearses are thumping and bobbing loosely.

14

Christopher Street? Do you hear me?
I have asked you to buy
your corpses which are beginning to look too beautiful

15

for the living to take,
aren't we sure this is true,
you and I? The Women's Penitentiary is nodding, excluded

16

from the more generous trapeze,
that is, housing.
No! it is a far more liquid world we are wearing out

17

our sneakers on the trail of,
it is rather comic, the way
the attractions work and have worked up and down the sea,

18

and of course it's hooded
in the church of this amusement,
and they are ruining their furry little hearts' hearts.

[New York, June 1953]

Bridlepath

It was quiet in the old house.
The plants were all upstairs
        and it was sunning.
There was gin somewhere but who can find it?
At the edge of the white forest they saw
the old house, the house of that part.
Well it was never so rundown, but it
        was shelter
and they looked so lovely in its lavender.
They talked all the time of "the eve"
and as they rocked and creaked they swore
        but so softly. In the air
the house had continually renewed itself
up the hill until it looked quite haggard,
and it looked newer this way which depressed
the considerate tourists who never whittled
the trees any more because the house looked
more interesting, blue with the shadow of twigs.
        Something is going to happen,
but they won't be walking this way.

Indian Diary

This morning the thatchers came.
Wowkle put her feet in the grey water
and waded songfully. "Oh heron, rise ..."
The beavers thought she was my daughter
and didn't swim, hung there, the same
up and down the banks, all eyes.

In early light my fleas look pink.
They smell me up and don't even bite
much any more, one got stuck in the grease
on my hair, I saw in the stream my white
part and it struggling. I don't think
the Wabanakis settle in our peace,

they mean to fight us at night, let
them, it is good. "Woman will watch"
and hold out a hand at dawn, so brave
disaster may not fail to find this scratch
in the sky signal to send an amulet
of rude flesh to the dad, the warm grave.

Why I build, why they build, at home
the woman always will know where she goes
and then come back to me and remember me
here by the waters, whether cold arrows
have flung themselves into my narrow blood, foam
has poison fought to the roof of my mouth. See:

"Came water. Rise, daughter!" Same eyes,
pink. "Bite grease. White think peace,
let watch brave. Scratch amulet." Grave,
home goes me. "Arrows! Foam, see."

[New York, July 1953]

"Light Conversation"
a recording by Gold and Fizdale

"Apricots! parishes!
is the palace burning?"
two pianos were wading in the river.
"Is it a trading post?"

"At dusk we dove
into an hexagonal pool
in the black-leafed wood-hole."
"Are you out fruiting?"

"My dear Tartar,
but aren't you Alsatian,
though! in the middle of winter
you find a loaf

and it's full of lilacs."
"Can't you keep your eyes off them?"
"O my dear two-headed,
don't be a monster!"

[New York, July 1953]

Southern Villages, a Sestina

Captivating in its immortal fragrance!
the Lending Library duskily stands,
a cannibal at either side of its lips
proudly alert and cocking both their ears.
And in the deepest light they read book
after book with their heavy-lidded eyes.

One of their mottoes cries "Oh eyes!
isn't it due to your peculiar fragrance
that we buy and sell at roadside root-beer stands?
that we buy and sell until our lips
loose their hold on money?" The ears
of the Library resound to a motto, not a book.

Well but why not? What's in a book?
And isn't the librarian full of eyes?
watching the adolescents with their familiar fragrance
passing each other in between the stands.
She spies what's trembling on their lips
and tries to clap her hands over their ears.

Yes, she is really interested in ears,
and she will not just issue you a book.
"How many dates have you contracted with your eyes?"
asks she, before dispensing a similar fragrance
and getting an enormous fish down from the stands.
She is also interested in lips.

She learned to read first with her lips,
then suddenly the world was full of ears
as if they were horses reading a book
and, walking into the Library, their eyes
glazed, like a music that enchanting fragrance
circled where a student black-and-whitely stands.

"They are practicing pianos in Paris, but stands
our Lending Library yet!" in a world of lips
following rather too close for comfort upon ears.
Oh valiant despite the dullness of each book,
disreputable and shy before all eyes,
"Terrible eyes! closed to the Library's filial fragrance,"

her fragrance zooms while the Library stands
with its carnivorous lips pressed to both his ears,
He takes the book out, lets her kiss his heavy-lidded eyes.

[Sledens Landing, September 1953]

Green Words, a Sestina

First I filled the chair with grapes
then I sat down on the sun
to watch a tree like moss escape the sky.
The cat watches me write and the cat
purrs blackly along the leaf, the strokes
which are a mystery to him and to me.

The cat finds everything mysterious but the sun,
how he purrs and claws just to watch the sky!
to lick the pen, to lie on the belly of a cat
and have it interrupt your strokes,
and push the French books into me,
which is like moss and is grapes,

isn't that what you think of the sky?
as your white-clad ankles are scratched by the cat.
You continue as long as you can your strokes
before a white scream comes out of me
and I sit on the grapes
accidentally. It does feel like the sun,

I am pushed into the sun by a cat.
The terrible black lashings! then the strokes
which are a mystery to him and to me.
The cat finds everything mysterious but the grapes,
and now me. "Yes, it does feel like the sun,"
I say, "the sun in the sky."

I look out over the river and the strokes
are white, they no longer hurt me.
I am bruised and acrid like the grapes
lying messily in the sun.
I no longer see any trees in the sky.
It is because I am deserted by the black cat,

his cool yellow eyes. He has left me.
Tears are breaking over me like grapes.
It is the sun.
O brilliant eyes escaping into the sky!
You are white, you are no longer cat,
why are you wet with strokes?

The grapes are drying in the sun.
And the sky is its own black cat
which it strokes, as it does me.

[Sledens Landing, August 1953]

Tschaikovskiana

1
A sniper walks in the woods.
Snow settles on his gun barrel
like the left hand of a swan.
O head-dress of many colors!
you are full of brambles,
you are a flight of arrows,
you are a mere ribbon on a harp,
you are an avalanche!
and through it as through a wedding
we see the smiling Viennese actress.

2
O Volga! you've poured yourself into my hands!

3
Someone is wetting the decks.
Someone is accompanying on the cello.

The Cossacks are arriving by freight train.
The peasants are selling their chewing gum.

Volodya get off your knees,
I am wetting my pants, oh redness
sitting on a carved chair, aren't you
Evgeni dying? oh immortal wound!

Something is backing up along the tracks.
Something is starving in the fragile oats.

4
Ring out, bells! It is Easter.
I am morning. Is that clear? Ah!
consumption, you are the pillow of desire.

Palisades

1

Driving in the morning to the city
men building a new road
we wait by them for the dynamite
to raise earth and rock a short way
slowly in the air, the dust
after we go on to the bridge
a reddish bloom on the hood.

2

What color is the river?
The risen sun is striking it.
Mercurially
it flows to flee
the blows of light
the sun rains on it.
What color is the river?

3

A short walk from the car
fragrant and wintry
a white moon through twigs

a minute or less to the house
on the evening of the first day
of all the leaves fallen

onto the fields, lawns and road
and a few into nests
that can at last be counted

Bill's Body Shop

Oh snows of only two months ago!
when will you fall back up into the sky
and fall down again like an airplane?

I put my passengers onto the plane
and then drove back to Palisades in the car,
the Palisades all hoary with the tears,

and left a check with a note, Bill
being out, "Fix up the car and fix up
my heart, the thirty dollars is for that,"

but the mechanics couldn't find the
trouble, so how could they fix it up? Oh
saffron snows! leaves tumbling, two months!

and I never saw that car again, No,
I don't remember the license number either.
I remember the elephants passing, and snow.

A Little on His Recentness

1
Now that I am leaving Bayswater
I may as well review my swims.
You are inescapable, my nudes in the golden,
and where you thought there was
a mirror it was only me, leaving.

2
But in the same canto, snow
was mentioned, I forget in what
context. The epic was wrenched from
my ring-covered hands! so I took off
my rings, laid them on the ebony
taffrail, and began to sing into the wake.

3
I wonder if Margaret is still alive?
People who are dying make that power
very intense while they can, but they can
do very little and it's the end; and we
are notified; or we are not notified, O scar.

4
No. I am always with you,
with your brooding Ekaterinburg looks;
something was settled in my heart
and it was not a farm or the borshch,
or an engine leaving the station
its "Aha!" in its cloud of soot.

[There's Such an I Love You!]

There's such an I love you!
no fainting pearl so delicate,
Bobby, as if a rumor were scented,
never there, yet, always here.

He opens like a flower and like a
flower never looks away from me,
it is the Kiss of the Snow Maiden.
the Smile of the famous Golden Forest.

Poem

Water flow strongly O clouds
O heavy coursing of my blood
which is like a powerful intellectuality
of words lost in the sea's crashing

And then faster and faster
the saline gushes of knowledge

To be alone
is the meaning of meaning O sand
the single mouth howling
its simple moonlike pain
until it too is crushed and filled
with the all-encompassing passions
which know everything

Dear Bobby

It seems that we are not apart.
Since you have gone the sullen heart
's made no discoveries and the time
of day's not hateful, not sublime,
it just keeps falling in a heap
between each vacant thundering sleep.

    Chaucer calls this illness
    Troilus' simple tears;
    it thrives in utter stillness
    and nourishes my fears.

I wonder if this will see you
before you leave for Corfu,
will your lips say this in Paris
which I love to so embarrass?
You must pardon love my mood
which is dolorous and crude

    and would be a subtle shout
    of breath upon your thighs,
    whose banner's "The Without"
    while bereaved of your dark skies.

            Love,
            Frank

                  [November 23, 1953]

To Bobby

On your head a white plant sits of thought
and you nag your beast of freshness still
sitting on the prong of a trapeze in the aisle
taming and yet mawling the elevated night.

Cars surround the cinders and freezes
the bravos have failed to relieve you, my dear,
and like a tulip your bed repossesses you where
my surging airiness no longer tumbles

Accustomed to what impulsive caress
do your limbs quicken against the hot statues
course to you like a wave in bondage
and arrive to emblazon you with my tongue

Passion of Alps and surmounting azure
and the revelations of tumultuous forests
their fire is merely the sweat of my knees
for I am your spring I am who you drink

[New York, November 1953]

[So the Spirit of Music, the Cascades!]

So the spirit of music, the cascades!
the roulades! the sick flesh and the art!
takes you gently by the throat
and forces you to the freshly washed window
where the brilliant November air
lays bare that backbone which will deck,
in a moment! oh vile horns! oh lust!
the triumphantly delicate neck
of the courtyard like a piece of lint.

Sonnet

O at last the towers!
that pierce the steaming sky,
I love power.

The marble is golden with love
and each crane is hot
in the clouds.

These swollen towers pulse
with music and are hard,
like the heart,

and I swear on the horizon
of years of thinking of
you and New York.

Are you merciful?
Yes, I am your will.

[A Face over a Book]

A face over a book
and then parting.

The green roofs,
the stone lions,

a simple sentence
lingers on the streets

as snow comes
to the hushed ear.

Where am I?
A windowpane shatters;

the sun has never
come out for me,

and my books
turn red with air.

[New York, December 1953]

132

[Into the Valley They Go]

Into the valley they go
bay withers, black flanks;
and the riders smile below

as they simulate ranks
and disfigure the quiet snow.
They climb into their tanks

and become the interminable foe
like a waterproof belt of banks
as the stammering barrels sow.

[New York, December 1953]

[She Hefted Her Leg onto the Table and]

1. She hefted her leg onto the table and
sneezed. She was on the cover of *Life* once.
It is a banjo filled with gum.

2. The grass grew taller around the banjo.
"Stranger escapes monument" cried the newsboys.
And the world began to play with itself.

3. A map decided it would present *The Messiah*
on Sunday, in an arrangement for banjo.

On a Back Issue of *Accent*

Then after years I found your stories
Someone said "Limpid. He's really more of
a prose writer than a poet, isn't he? I've
never read his verse and liked them."

More what than what? my darling soul!
whose love I must always move in slowly
like a file of soldiers in the declivity
which rests them and saves them from enemy fire.

And in this valley of your nature I too find
the earth most beautiful around me.

The Last Day of the Zoo
to Helen Parker

1   Guanaco

"Have you been to the fame-house?" Pearls!
Asparagus tips! O blue shingles, O rats.
"Yet to be miserable is at least to be here,
far from Washington. I smell the seats."

They were witnessed fiercely by amber churls
caught up in the diligence of publicity. Green,
the vast swards of a remembered cafeteria, a tear
floated on her breast, poor May. "This is spleen
in the afternoon, damn it." And now, were
they watching, the snarl would be still of a country
regret, full of cloves and Woodmere. "You girls
don't color your ears. She has a run." Tree.

2   Kangaroo

"You, who was enamored of me at the trough
last week, did you see me spit into the wind?
Glorious moment of defiance! I thought I'd lost
my marbles. The merest hank of a regret is enough
to make me run to you like a Laplander at Easter.
My eyes are red from reading. I didn't shave
this morning, I was that distracted by the snow."

And the leaves came down and down, like memories
of past happiness, the more thought of the more dry
and tough. As if the aborigines hadn't been possible,
so completely were they rehearsed and rerehearsed.
There was, too, an impossibility of mountains and grass
which was incomparably withered by the intransigence
of this pouchy beautiful mind's nostalgia. Gulf.
"And had you been reading Lyof?" Wrinkled lips,
huddling in the doorway of the Brazilian Embassy.

3   Zebra

The mesmerization of flight. Lost pocketbooks.
"Was that Colonel Lindbergh?" Warm golden seals
shaking their bracelets at the kites. An enormous hardoy
thrusting its black look into the cemetery. Wizards
on ostriches were singing *Last Rose of Summer*
as we rounded up the novels of Upton Sinclair
and extended them like a shawl over the freezing students.
Saigon had never looked more department-store,
all careless and bathetic, like a pill on a tongue,
"and the two green birds will be forever parted
by their ability to know and to feel extremities."
It's like the case history of a movie star that flopped

135

called "Dodo Mac Dougal," who spoke French too well.
Everything finds its right place I don't think, you thief.
Zippers crashing into the flea-house at midnight.
The filibuster will again become a palace but we won't
be in it, O my sultan, my beautiful sad dark friend.

4   Shopper

So the world's become generous
        time of the Whip
very proud of the envious
        white of their lip

undecided and dear; dear,
        not quite animal
any more, because the year
        's become general

and all the buildings fall
        on the tired feet;
and the wind comes, the natural,
        to the last sweet

frightened pig who isn't
        ready; as the heart
knows what it knows and isn't,
        and tries to be art.

[1953]

To the Meadow

You have been evil and blue-green
    you have filled me with venomous scowls
you have worked upon me as a scene
    in which faces were smothered in towels.

You have held me as they held me
    whom I loathe beyond my powers
and I remember that you felt me
    worth twenty-four of your hours;

though would sweetly sing again
    to grassy brookward watch you drown
O filthy connoisseur! where you'd been
    you'd go, rushing toward the town.

And then the love I felt for you
    would move me as it moved before
over this meadow's light dew
    and trembling, freshening floor.

I am not ingenuous yet
    to pluck you your eyes or flowers,
my broken heart is in your debt
    and it will mend—a few hours.

[New York, January 1954]

Benjamin Franklin,
or Isadora Duncan

It seems that I'm carrying a cloud
in my arms, and it's crying. Do we
only live to be fifty so we can say
"His silver cranium, heart! bursts,
doesn't, o children, do you love him?"
Anxiety, they say, never knew him,
he was like a basket before it.

Ambassadors! are you allowed to be
elegant or forced? Are you as dramatic
as the fourth of something? Did you
rub Robespierre? A century of fainting
and carting, and then a war over tin.
The terracotta landscape with wind,
its luminous purse trod by fauns.

Yes, I want school children to love
in a long solo the sheer French of it,
and you, dear bulge of urbanity. Is
the currency becoming more decorative?
You'd look more bored in hyacinths.
A long history of affection and regret.
I'm hiding under your wrinkled mountain.

[Southampton, January 1954]

138

Augustus

Jet pears hung squalidly against the drapes
and his fingertips glistened with frost.
The orange sun melted his nape.
In his drafty palace, there lived a statue
and over the palace Augustus sent his vines,
cerise cries in the white air.
Tender little shots rang out.

Waterfalls swelled and kissed before him,
knelt and screamed as crowns spun
through the night, the night of Augustus
which was like an army of marauders,
unceasing and full of insight,
the dashing snow! the pure! the fierce! the free!
and the waterfalls were still as flames.

The voices began, like so many daggers.
At first Augustus only felt them
as doves attempting to hide in his breast,
but soon they surrounded him completely
like a crown of screams, as clearly as sand
pouring through glass in the winter desert.
He was the metal of his crown at last.

Poem

The paralysis of power and ease
has accomplished this city
                    or it is a fist.

The Mike Goldberg Variations

1

Here is the country with its houses full of red paint
and grey shingles and the clear yellow paper of the sky.
"Painter sells painting to Providence Museum in February"
says the local Thursday newspaper with a knowing eye.
    O golden mountain, yellow as a thigh!

To fame! to fortune! to the modest whim of the public air
which has everything it needs including blue, clouds and mouths
agape, we offer our tensile wrists strong as granite,
slender as wiry palmettos rattling in the innumerable Souths.
    O golden mountain, perilous to youths!

I walk the country in wet shoes while you are in the quarry,
oh New York! under the same sun which is whiter there
and blue at night, and has its own Venetian enemy at sundown
where the clouds rush across the Battery into the Atlantic's chair,
    O golden mountain, glistening like hair!

2

The air is warm, the sand
is wet and this is smaller
than it need be; this is last
if not least. To be taller,
    O golden mountain, youthful as desire for pain!

                      is to go away and therefore
                      have to come back, unless you are
                      the local color in your public
                      life. There's a place like a star,
    O golden mountain, gracious peril of the thigh!

which is no longer there; but
the stones of painting are very much
like the stones of Venice, no
matter the newspapers and the clutch,
　　O golden mountain, yellow as a beagle's eye!

　　　　　　　　　　of prurience. It's to be there
　　　　　　　　　　and to be cut like all the other
　　　　　　　　　　rocks. While here the foolish
　　　　　　　　　　dog thinks I'm its brother,
　　O golden mountain, perfect as the glistening rain!

　　　　　　　　　　　　　　[Southampton, March 1954]

Room

The steamboats sank in the river
and over it an orange legend sighed.
"Chairs! chairs! why must you sink?"

Before autumn had raffled off its roses
I swam out to the buoy and cut myself
like the time I kissed the unicorn.

With sweaters and in flannels I bought
the river, its flaccid smile was mine at last!
and my wristwatch became rusty with happiness.

　　　　　　　　　　　　　　[New York, March 1954]

[Dumb Urns in Sycamore Temples]

Dumb urns in sycamore temples
cerebrate the birth of the Infant Cigarette
and I march for years of silver
towards this herbaceous cognizance.

The knowledge of divinity
is pressed upon my brow like spring garlands
of myrtle glistening with urine.
O prolong yourself, oily tenderness!

and the communication of this
is an outrage to those who have no tongues—
of course, I shall be deposited
upon the pyre of my fatally deliberate kisses

which were given to avert, I swear it!
this fatal catastrophe of the turbines:
on their knees they are imagining that they are
trees. There is nothing more vestal.

[New York, March 1954]

Lexington Avenue, an Eclogue

AMYNTAS: O mournful sunset, I have lost
  my sheep with the wandering blush
  of the sun that would not linger
  on my cheeks, not beyond noon ...

DORIS: Sheep? you mean you've lost your
  love, don't you? and your penis
  is showing. Put that bunch of grapes
  back on your lap. Just for dignity.

AMYNTAS: Now that I am entirely disrobed
  you feel flippant, don't you?

DORIS: It's a compliment from me, don't
  mistake my informality for disinterest ...

AMYNTAS: or do you expect me to forget the
  cares of the day as soon as your eyes

DORIS: Never mind my eyes!

AMYNTAS: open? It must
  be the cocktail hour or you wouldn't
  be up.

DORIS: I've been up since dawn.

AMYNTAS: No.
  You are the dawn.

DORIS: Tee hee. I expected
  you to take that tack. If you don't
  understand something, you say I am it.

AMYNTAS: Where are my beautiful sheep which
you do not believe in? I worry. Are
their delicate legs, somewhere, twisted?

DORIS: I don't disbelieve them, I've just
never seen them. You are very critical.

AMYNTAS: I offer you these arms which have
protected animals, and these thighs
which have bumped them, and these lips
which have loved them as I love you.

DORIS: And I accept the man, for who
does not love all, cannot love me,
though it pains me not to be unique
and I would be the only animal
who ever rested, bleating, in your arms.

AMYNTAS: But do you sense a terrible feeling
in the West?

DORIS: But do you love me
least?

AMYNTAS: I love you only, though I
watch out for lots. For instance,
have you ever seen a sonata?

DORIS: They
say the sheep are always describing

AMYNTAS: Well not to me!

DORIS: a sonata. Can it be
the lost sonata?

AMYNTAS: Can it be the lost
subway?

DORIS: Why aren't you more serious?

AMYNTAS: I'm too worried about my duties
as a shepherd, and besides, lust
makes one frivolous.

DORIS: Oh does it? lust?

AMYNTAS: You are describing my inner nature.

DORIS: You are describing me with your arms.

AMYNTAS: I am in love.

DORIS: I am in love with you.

AMYNTAS: You are becoming everything to me.
I love you more than duty, most
for looks, and more than hillsides
covered with their own plangent fragrance
which is just as much from bottles.

DORIS: You adore me, don't you?

AMYNTAS: Like
an animal!

DORIS: I am a pasture for your
flocks.

AMYNTAS: And I am grazing o'er
your citified blue locks

BOTH: which now
are heaven in the metropolitan gaze,
for all that's duty and desire is dust.

[New York, April 14, 1954]

[In the Pearly Green Light]

In the pearly green light
of early morning when dread
of day and some distant event
is just breaking off my head

of dreams and the security
of nightmares where a note
of myself is always throbbing
its characteristic rote

of personal anxiety, I wake
to real fears of war and chance
and, worse, of duty to the dead.
Yet I never wholly fear the romance

of my interior self no matter
how asleep I am, how nearly dead.

[New York, April 15, 1954]

Poem

Here we are again together
as the buds burst over the trees their
light cries, walking around a pond in yellow weather.

Fresh clouds, and further
oh I do not care to go!
not beyond this circling friendship,
damp new air and fluttering snow
remaining long enough to make the leaves
excessive in the quickness of their mild return,
not needing more than earth and friends to see the winter so.

[April 15, 1954]

[Pussywillows! Oh You're Still Here . . .]

Prelude

Pussywillows! oh you're still here, in a bottle of water grown green
with scum, near the bust and out the window in the fashionable sunshine.

Yes, electric charms, speaking always. A green radiator with a black
top below the dirty window sill.

Waltz

The face of my clock is the face of New York, isn't it? bought late in
April, early in March. Bloomingdale's. Beacon Ace. The E. Ingraham Co.,
Bristol, Conn., USA. Oh) Ingraham Co., made in Bristol, Conn., USA, S
to F, Time, Alarm. Always at it! and the synthetic aura of 5 minute coffee,
that Romanticism, tasting of lips and of brown morning whiskey.

Passacaglia

[New York, April?, 1954]

148

Movie Cantata

Prelude

I

Narrator: A great silver light appeared on the horizon, narrowed its eye to a pin point, and fell upon my breast, sobbing. What giggles! they were so intelligible I blushed. There, lying among the hairs on my chest, was this tiny jewel, pendant.

Other voice: It's always embarrassing to see.

Narrator: Was it an opal? was it a wrist watch?
           Had it been returned?

Singer: No!
           It was me! It was the movies!

     Recitative: O brilliant era! you have again commenced! There you are in your darling square black hat with the tassel that hides one eye. How many lives will enter that eye as if it were an observatory, stay in that eye as if it were a bank job, and end up in the heavens,
           alone, grey, but at least visible!
        I have not regrets, I assume responsibility for
                     those starlets.

   Aria:

[O Resplendent Green Sea! I Slowly Pierce]

O resplendent green sea! I slowly pierce
you like a minnow, and my strength seems narrow,
like the muscle in the arm of a child that
twitches, then is still. Your smile! so yes
infinitely cold, I am like a wire vibrating,
and like a smile thrashing across the face
of a sufferer, gasping for breath as he
reads. My immense jubilation, divine singularity!
scream thrust earthward on the glacial face
with sandsharks and stingrays in its frozen
glance! And I, my leaf in the century-long breakers,
toss, toss up my little O of foam, and sink.

[Southampton, May 1954]

[Five Sobs Lined up on the Doorstep]

Five sobs lined up on the doorstep
and one said "Is he blond and has he
blue eyes?" and another said "You do
well to cry, you won't see him again"
and another said "With your own blue
eyes, ha ha!" and another said "Be
glad he'd gone before you got too upset"
and another said "I'm in sympathy
with you, aren't you?" But it was rain.

[Southampton, May 1954]

Epigram for Joe

Here is the edge of the water where
the delicate crabs drift like shells;
stick in your purple toe "I've been swimming
for hours, it's freezing!" and is it,
with all the salt falling like
a fountain across your mottled flesh,
each curling hair unguently draped by
the shivering sun, pushed by short breezes
into a molding for your hot heart, a wire
basket. And where the sands sting you
they gleam like matchsticks in the noon.
You are standing in the doorway on the
green threshhold while it licks feet
that are burning to spread and flutter.

[New York, June 1954]

Ode

I don't eat wheat
and I wear my violin strings
around my neck in case I need them

Snow is being sent from the mountains
I lie down like the flowers
it is an elevator shaft, this island

Sweet nursery rhyme describing manna
and how far away all that is good is
and music, too

when I am absent weeps
as if the children overburdened
by my incessant playing

Oh heart described
you are being pushed out of existence
by a mysterious swelling

Men are angels

[New York, July 1954]

Jackie

(After John Gower)

There was once, as is gossipped,
a baseball player never whipped;
he was screamed by every fan,
every day he louder ran,
single, powerful and black,
he could bat: he was called Jack.
Brave by day, and delirious
by night or what's more serious
he lusted after myriads
of blondes; yet at periods
he longed to pick for fun, one
from out the wealth he'd won
of golden spirits at his feet
who adored him that he's fleet
and so brutish with the ball.

He was master of them all:
not deciding, yet dismayed
that no one face could be said
to depict his whole desire
though each eager as the fire.
He rode home in Cadillacs,
lonely, feeling that the lacks
of the Life of Fame adored
left him handsome, nervous, bored.
To Casinos and to bridge,
later on e'en to Oak Ridge:
he knew why atomic fission
and roulette was to his vision
tic-tac-toe; still he sought

love, considering he ought.
Now we know a great athlete
with a drunkard can't compete
for relaxation; from the fiend
's flying carpet he's been weaned:
from ambition's wild increase
he seeks amorous surcease.
Thus distracted Jackie came
to the plate and lost the game.
Twas the ultimate of the series
and gave rise to certain queries.

He had recently deposited
some money he'd had closeted
by betting underground and high:
the police thought they knew why.
Jackie said it was a loan;
the police said he had thrown
the game. And into darkest jail
threw Jackie trembling like a quail,
or a thoroughbred racehorse.

He read there some stories Norse
and in one of them it claimed
that no matter how much blamed
innocents would all get out.
Jackie cried, "Let Jackie out!"
and his tears? they brought the knout
(he'd been extradited then
to a vicious Southern Pen
where as little limitation
on guards as on the plantation
was imposed to spare his race.
They did spare Jack's handsome face,

though). Afterwards a nymph
with an ill disposèd lymph
at his cell window late peered:
she was everything Jack feared,
"Now, alas, the last disgust
of all those I sought in lust!
she's the vile hysteric terror
of the love I sought to mirror!
death runs fast on flagellation,
I dying pardon her elation."

"No! listen to my song!
I am virtuous, though wrong
in the head, and love you dearly.
I once studied with Miss Brierly.
will you marry me some time
if I tell you how to climb
o'er this hideous retribution?
Your own beauty's the solution,
but an intimate detail
is left out of that Norse tale!"
Yet how can he? how can Jackie
jump from prison to be lackey
in the heart of this blue witch
with her henna hair, her twitch?
Still, he'll die of malnutrition,
athlete's foot or parturition
if he doesn't reach the sun
before January One.

"Yes, I'll do it!" Brave decision,
trained in baseball. Does derision
smile behind her eager laugh?
And then too, his friends will scoff.

She says, "Darling, you've relations
who own several thousand Haitians.
Don't you think that family pride
ought to call them to your side?
And the Ball Club that you played for,
won't they see that it is paid for?
What? Why, darling, what? The Bribe!
to the D.A. they'll subscribe!
I will set the wheels in motion
with the energy of an ocean.
As you languish in this place
fondly think on faithful Grace,
the most loyal of your fans
who may someday bear you swans."
Was there very much to choose?
Life with her would be The Blues.
With supernatural rapidity
he was strolling through the city.
She was strolling on his arm
hidden by a whole mink farm.

But the day drew steadily dreader:
smiling Jackie'd bravely wed her.
All life's beautiful things he'd lost!

On their wedding night he tossed
from the bedroom to the bed,
from the bed into his head
crept green fantasies of death
and be couldn't control his breath
while the cheering of his fans
beat his ears like flying swans.
So ashamed that he could not
he flung up his hands and sought

her face. She spoke. "The light, Jack,
please turn on but turn your back."
Softly on his nape a breeze
sighed like palm oil; turns to seize
the most beautiful of his dreams.
In an ecstacy of sweat he streams
and shouting asks her if she's real.

"Try me, if I do not feel
like the Desdemona yours.
I'm the trumpet of your course.
Had I come to you like this
we would never have reached bliss!
for you never could decide
so my beauty I did hide.
Now I see by your great eyes
you will love me like the skies,
I will make all your desserts
and cheer for you in your shirts
as your international fame
seems to us a prison game."

[Southhampton, August 19, 1954]

157

[The Brittle Moment Comes]

The brittle moment comes
when you clutch the last of the grapes
and with depressing accuracy
the clouds slow down.

A boy drops his marbles
and suddenly the surface of the pool
collapses into noisy laughter
We look like dead leaves.

[1954]

[On the World's First Evening]

1
On the world's first evening
how evenly the light is falling!

it learned to fall so easily,
after a day full of lightning.

Now the rose will be created
so one night it may be blasted,

and the enormous Milky Way
bares a glittering bosom in that night,

she is leaning forward at the opera
and we stare up from the parquet.

2
Your flesh is familiar,
O night sunk in the perfume of clouds!
wandering in spacious loneliness
like so many exiled Popes.
You are their breath, night, while they pray,
you are the love we run from, through the day.

3
Trees breathe softly in your hair

F#

Drops of snow in
the month of May
and the falling nails,

the whispers,
the asparagus,
Cassell's New German Dictionary

asked me to come
and I came over and said
"Will you dance with me?"
because there's a floor
and I want to move.

As the windows
rattle against summer,

land seeing itself
for the first time
crying "Whiskey!"

[Now It Seems Far Away and Gentle]

Now it seems far away and gentle
the morning miseries of childhood
and its raining miseries over the schools

Alterable noons of loitering
beside puddles watching leaves swim
and reflected dreams of blue travels

To be always in vigilance away
from the bully who first broke my nose
and so I had to break his wristwatch

I hit him
        it fell off
                I stepped on it
and he
        will never again know
                    the time

A surprising violence in the sky
inspired me to my first public act
nubile and pretentious but growing pure

As the white-caps are the wind's
but a surface agitation of the waters
means a rampart on the ocean floor is falling

All will soon be open to the tender
governing tides of a reigning will
while alterable noon assumes its virtue

[Guston: Painting, 1954]

160

Corresponding Foreignly

1

You may flaunt my looseness, you know
that I go whole weeks without so, I
get depressed because I'm so easily distracted
from sex. It's not something you can keep
your mind on without losing it.

2

Certain eases appeal to me more than the flowering quinces
and your black pear branches dripping white petals.
I'm not a pastoral type any more, I take the subway
back and forth from beds to days or bed-in-the-day-time
and if pleased am a dirty flower at the end of ragtagging
it. "I hear you were down town last night. It was just like
old times." What a thing to say in an elevator. I'd feel
rather more assured, though, if we were rolling in a field
screaming above the records and the Japanese lanterns.
I hate the country and its bells and its photographs.

3

When he went west we thought he'd be big in the movies
with his humanity kick. The others went off to another party
but we went home and forgot each other in a good talk.
Then the radiators cracked and puffed and it did get warmer
but I dreamt of an anxiety the size of a public building,
something to race your car in and waken echoes. Did
you mention that you saw me dancing with a sculpture last week
in the Bowery? It was an audition and we called ourselves "The
                                                    Bananas."

4

Four little rats came into the house
because it had grown so cold out,
and they knew they'd be allowed the run
of our lives in the winter
when the weather doesn't favor them.

5

I met him in Los Angeles
and after weeks of feverish love
couldn't remember what he looked like
if he was farther away than the john.

I wondered what he had done
to me. He was like a shrike.
I don't know if it was really love
and he's left Los Angeles.

6

I have a tic of thinking about it, if
they can really fine you for paying the rent
late. His photograph would have to be moved
to a new building, and by now it's the size
of a mural. It would take weeks. I won't.

Song

J'arrive au casserole et je casse une croûte
elle est un frémissement cataire à moi
je suis aveugle, catéchisation sans doute
j'ai peur et je ne peux pas apprendre cette loi

O misères du Christianisme exemplaire
qui marchent et marchent surtout comme un enfant
—dites-vous elles sont vis-à-vis la bestiaire
et, donc, se noyent dans un font rouge et charmant?

Ce Christ mange toute la ville, la ville est tout
qui arrive en casserole et qu'il la casse une croûte

[May 6, 1955]

Bagatelle, or the Importance of Being Larry and Frank

How cheerful it is to be weeping in the springtime!
our enemies have labeled us (O' Miz miz)
and don't they file suits against Europa and
pretend they are the soldiers of joy?
We were thinking of many other things, ta rah!
(when the cops ran into the Alpine—a building)
and school let out; it was time to go to the movies.
Ugh affair. Oh affair. Was there a funeral to attend?
Did you think you were creating your own hormone shots?
Did you think you didn't think. The beast is at last a bore,
I wanted to tell the bull something but he went.
The bald hills absorbed his semen. He swam in the grass.
They keep blaming her for riding away on him.
"I'm tired of imitating those whom I no longer respect."
Does the city think of itself as dark and cloudy? Dogs!

Their life had raised the level of their countrymen
to a giggle in a urinal. O Hall of Mirrors!
(I asked a law to kill the O!) The most pickled
of the works of the past was denied jury and information.
Denied the podium the actors graced the cafeterias.
They were waiting for a lunch messenger with serious brows
He would give the high sign and die of honesty.
And it would be no empty gesture, the mush mouth,
"Someday he'll be a board of Aldermans"
for him to continue to address the cafeterias of this world
which have grown girlish a place to salute chopped liver.
But we feel one way about folly and another about out and out
mature boys. "It works" "It doesn't work" Like crows
and it is tiring to make balloons out of rubber bands
or to hear "Auntie" caught in "and the." Matta lives in Venice.

"Hello, I'm Mark Rothko's mother."

Pitcher

Leaning from her balcony the senile laundress
exclaims over aviators, grounded, their wrists
a whole hairy bicycle racing her vertigo.

There are not many balconies in America,
a provincial passion pretending to be desperate
in goggles at ruby moments, aloft. She sighs

and wrings her hands at the pathetic hoax
of it, "them up there and them down here," all
so purple in her spinning blood-flecked eyes,

iron spokes pressing her belly that if she fall,
swoop into the steaming paradise of dusk,
she will be held above the fire till night.

And if terrifying levitation should ensue
the aviators will press her back upon
the lunging trees. Negress, the snowing moon.

Collected Proses, an Answer

BUFFALO DAYS

Damned damage! Ugh, and this barbed wire tastes
    like feathers.

THE ORANGE WIVES

Idling along, I saw a muskrat kissing a mushroom in
    the merry autumn.

GREAT HUMAN VOICES

John L. Sullivan, Tiger Flowers, Dizzy Gillespie, oh
    Bobo Olson!

COLORFUL HOUR

In Scandinavia the raindrops are manicured.

EXPRESSION

Yeah!

SLEEP

At present writing *The Prodigal* starring Lana
    Turner has run for 30 seconds.

A MINERAL WICK

He went to sleep quickly in the garage, puffing away
    on his exhaustion.

SOMEWHERE

Baby Katherine is munching a little celluloid.

CECELIA
Play it, girl!

THE SILVER WORLD
Can I talk to you? Just let me talk to you! just for
a minute!

JEWELRY SEVENTHS
The automat sitting on the cloud, the airability of buns,
the green ohs.

AN ESKIMO COCA COLA
The Art Institute of Chicago has authorized me to change
you, dear.

THE EXCEPTION PROVES THE RULE
A glass palace : ripe pears : : Bobo Olson : The Silver
World.

THE WATER HOSE IS ON FIRE
Lake Superior lying across my shoulders, what maribou
scents!

THE LINGERING MATADORS
Babe, Lysistrata, Cutenick, Ambrose, the Duke and
Duchess of . . . eek!

EGYPT
Now let's not be too serious.

IS THERE A HOUSE INSIDE THAT FUEL ENGINE?
Yup.

WHY WEREN'T THEY MORE CAREFUL?
D.W. GRIFFITH CAUGHT ON FIR TREE ORGY
CLAIMS FIFTH AMENDMENT INVITATION!

PEANUT BUTTER CANDY
The sea lapping along, and then the laps seeing, and
the See collapsing.

THE BRINDLE COWS
Seriousness, to the King, meant next to nothing, I should
add here.

IN THE MERRY FOAM
Jane and Kenneth and Larry and Frank (Bill and Elaine
and Leo watching).

MY MIX-UP
I saw him at the dock. I saw her in the bar. I ate.
I wrote to Yaddo.

MILKWEED EMBLEMS
A sort of epithalamium mess they call them, oh hell,
they're brown.

SUPPOSE
Riding along with a song on your dong in the fong o'er
Hongkong.

THE GREEN MEDDLER
How serious *is* meddling?

A HOUSE IN MISSISSIPPI
I can read but I can't live, that's my trouble. Smell
      that wisteria?

WICKED OBJECTS
Honey bars, bears' toenails, ichthyology, pessimistic sur-
      prise, jewels.

FRESH LIMES
Say there, little girl blue, rinse your hair!

THE WINDOW
starring Arthur Kennedy, Ruth Roman, Barbara Hale
      and Bobby Driscoll.

PAINTED FOR A ROSE
Baby Katherine is only two weeks old. She loves wearing
      make-up.

NOONS
Yes, John, I'd love to lunch. No, it's too expensive.
      I hate it there, o.k.

ROOMS
Pressed against a pane of glass, the detective couldn't
      get his gun out.

IN THE RANCHHOUSE AT DAWN
Would you pass me that copy of *Two Serious
Ladies* over there on the bunk?

THE OUTSIDE OF THINGS

Intriguing, what? then we went motoring, and THEN
        we went home together through the tires.

THE BLACK LION

"How much?" "Nothing." "What good is it then?"
        "It's fun." "Oh yeah?"

IN THE COAL MUD

It's heaven! It's like reading Gérard de Nerval for the
        last time.

THE HAND-PAINTED EARS OF DEATH

The rancher didn't think he'd remember him, but there
        he was right smack dab in the way again, bucking
        and snorting like a woman.

ALABAMA

All this is Alabama at dawn in the muddy ranchhouse
        seriously painting jewelry in the window of foam.

[June 30, 1955]

Une Journée de Juillet

My back is peeling and the tar
melts underfoot as I cross the street.
Sweaty foreheads wipe on my shirt
as I pass. The sun hits a building
and shines off onto my face. The sun
licks my feet through my moccasins
as I feel my way along the asphalt.
The sun beams on my buttocks
as I outdistance the crowd. For a
moment I enter the cavernous vault
and its deadish cold. I suck off
every man in the Manhattan Storage &
Warehouse Co. Then, refreshed, again
to the streets! to the generous sun
and the vigorous heat of the city.

[July 12, 1955]

[Dusk. Dawn. The Land.
An Albatross Thinks of Spain.]

Dusk. Dawn. The land. An albatross thinks of Spain.
In the center the red diamond grins meanly. I
am going to surrender the Armed Forces.
You hear the grass walking by.
Eyes the color of black coffee. The will
is a very strong swimmer, freshly greased.
A tired hand is laid across the railroad tracks.

Attacca

To take up where you left off!
without a breath of separation
your new movement is begun.
The heart pulses on, developing
a future. You do not rest
your lips, your ears, your fingers.
The field is full of daisies
And the sun is shining greenly.
It is a musical development,
taxing and inspired, before
the old love has echoed away.
To the eager suggestion of a new
face. It will be a great movement!
begun warmly and without a pause.
You have carried yourself to a new
world, put off the final applause.

[March 1, 1956]

Chopiniana

Rooftops, miles of them, slate
and brick faces turned to the sky.
Night is falling and the snow,
and somewhere behind me, in this room
or is it behind another window behind
me? the revolutionary piano thunders.

Roofs, falling as the sky is falling,
and the world turns, desperately trying
to shake these faces from its face.
Snow is covering us like plaster. We
shall be here, as Warsaw, Moscow, Paris,
Rotterdam and even shy Vienna were there,
dying under the stormy, musical snow.

[She, Has She Bathed in Sound]

She, has she bathed in sound
as a cello opens itself to rain.
And manna falls on the sinner,
and snow falls on the starving.

With the savor of pain, she
has become a fountain. Poured
forth, as a virgin will love
and loving will move forward.

Draw, from this fountain, love
into your chambers. Not rejoicing,
but as wine is becoming to souls
and a window to life opens walls.

[March 21, 1956]

[It Is 1:55 in Cambridge,
  Pale and Spring Cool,]

It is 1:55 in Cambridge, pale and spring cool,
it is. Evenings in Jim's Place with Jimmy
and listening to Lenya sing all day long. Yes,
I would like another beer and Bert Brecht is
a great poet, and Kurt Weill, he is a genius too.
Most of all it is a gift from Wystan, Germany,
when years ago Storm Troopers came close
as a knock on our doors before we met, as
terrifying as a game at recess when the bullies
were on the other side. And when they were on
our side it was worse. And gradually fearing
disappeared in knowing, another gift from Wystan,
though it too was worse, for there is no paying
on both sides. And now it is almost the last hour
of your visit, Jimmy, no more walks by the Charles
"the alluvial river" drifting through a town
that's pretty because it is so flat. No more
great decisions on titles and places, no more
too many drinks. Will those poems ever get
written? will our royalties from VISITING
ANGKOR VAT AND VIENNA really sustain us, in a
future that only yesterday seemed so literally
bright? Goodbye. At least we've written our ODE.
And elsewhere, as snows dirty, we'll sit
for long long days and talk and play the phonograph
and heat the coffee. And silent, go to a bar.

[April 17, 1956]

To John Ashbery on Szymanowski's Birthday

Whitelight, keenair, someone
with a Polish accent: j'ai septembre,
et milles-fois-retours d'Ashes,
like so many violins, from Paris.

The memory of seven sickening seconds
at the top of Carnegie Hall, where
the bow was pulled of its horsehairs
and the insect suddenly started

humming, unwinding the silver cord
that binds the heart. That was
a concerto! simply-moving glacier
of northern sympathies, sliced banyans

wrapped in glistening green leaves,
lying in an enormous white freezing unit.
Did you practice the piano, John,
while you were gone? summoning thunder

as the delicate echoes of Slavic
nostalgia pretend to have defeated
Napoleon? and have, heaving into a
future of crystalline listening.

I am conducting you in his Symphonie
Concertante. Remember our successes
with the Weber Konzertstück? It is no
repetition, when the marvelous

is like taking off your earmuffs
at the North Pole. I am writing to invite
you to the Polish Embassy for cocktails,
on this superb fall day, musicien américain.

Poem

Flower! you are like synthetic feelings, full of
    tomorrow and yesterdays and Tuesday, you are
    loved by those who grew you,

but I loathe you, daffodil! I am green as the grass
    towards you and I loathe every crinkling senti-
    ment of your still-bulbous flesh.

O sun!

must you leave me here alone? Will you abandon me,
    and soon the forsythia will be out and everything
    will be yellow?

I am too late, from wandering; and grass is growing
    in my heart, the tough, indiscriminate grass
    which knows no color but the wind.

Un Chant Contre Paroles

What if one of us could be
                              the greatest lover in history
could one of us without the other
                    do it? I doubt it

        and so much has been written about us already

I have pursued you endlessly
                    beside a flowery stream
and you've won battles for me
                    before the flaming gates
we fornicated once in storms
                    lashed to the mast in sheets

and later you proudly showed me
                    the elephants' burial ground
the exact spot where Moses
                    received the tablets from the air
our consuming passion, you said
                    was knowledge and it was written down
someone was always listening
                    and through the long history of love
a volume of words moved
                    glacially between us
bearing to some distant shore
                    our mutual greenness and growth

it was you or me the Vikings
                        sailed for, and the English later smoked
all torn and burnt
                        the fragments of our joining
covered mountains up to the snow line
                        where the reindeer fed in winter
as once we each . . .
                        at war with one another we fell together
starting the Reconstruction Age
                        it's always been rather like spring, hasn't it?
and Roman poetry
                        an age of peace is terribly long and we
have lost each other, drawn
                        too far into the meaning of our legend
this hyacinth that greets me now
                        is it familiar?

        all I can remember is a French description of your eyes

[And Leaving in a Great Smoky Fury]

And leaving in a great smoky fury
of his loved ones, he sailed
backwards to Europe discovering islands,
the pale ones and the ones like
elephants and those like pearls.

But the trees shall stand never
so high as in his native land!
they hoped, but he found ruins and
aqueducts and fountains, and loved them.

[Three Parodies]

Post-Graduate (Ciardi)

I wonder why they sip and toddy still
in back of Beacon Hill
                    and tote their pain
into the swan-ridden Public Gardens
which has become a middle-brow Gardner's
because of the incessant shows of flimsy
abstractionists from Maine.
                        Their whims, he
divulges, intend to make them serious
instead of sober, the spokesman of their kind.

Then why write about Newport? and why
don't the swans bite and the ducks sit?
Have they been fed too much on rind? I . . .
                              It
seems a shame that a city with the best-run
hotel in America should be called "The Hub-Nun."

A Web of Saints Near the Sea (Lowell)

Life sappeth the spirit; and given the will to Paul,
I call upon Ignatius the Loyalist, the shriven of
the Lord, to beat a tambourine for Mother Ursuline. She,
profound Bun upon her nape, of crucified Christ
the memory and endorsement, is most apparent in high heels.
Then where the spirit that the Ghost adjured? O sitting
in far-off Rome among the Puritan responses, HE
whom almight and injustice sought the stain of to become
more human, is the curse of all who do not see as you and me,
for Genji spider sweeps the stairs that we walk up,
and he walks down, you needn't doubt, as great waves break.

Chestnut Eats Horse (Eberhart)

Laws govern boys in tents
and oh! the charming simples
that they learn. A fox comes in
and dies, and it is glittering.

Cool tears mature the rascal in the heart
and on the lake a storm comes up:
it is the horse's hooves, and summer
greets him like a god through fog.

I have seen the fog come in and I
have wondered. Were it a dog, then
dog were god, instead of fox or horse,
oh pain! so godless on the endless chain.

Yet is it light beneath and in
the chestnut of the heart, the lake
so clear and dappling yet with sorrow,
yet and yet, a poem and a simple leaf.

[October 21, 1957]

Episode

Dear: The Letter

The reason I loved you from the first moment we met is because you seemed to hold a certain hostility towards me which I mistook for wisdom. I thought you really knew me instinctively, which is a laugh. But who's laughing?

In the heyday of our exceptional excitement with each other I think you thought I loved you blindly, but actually I was just wondering whether you loved me or just saw through me to yourself. That, of course, is nothing to be sneezed at. I'm not saying that I didn't enjoy (*enjoy!* how cool I am!) sex with you more than *with* anyone else in my whole life so that it hardly seemed to be with anyone and became something else, like a successful American satellite, but the thought of it doesn't exactly nourish me spiritually.

Yes, it does. It would still keep me out of a monastery, if I were invited to attend one.

But this is a message, no time for thinking. The thinking's been done. By you too, baby. I didn't just make this all up. So now that you feel serious and responsible again, what do you propose to do about it? I'm not putting any return address on this, and it's being mailed by a "friend" so don't count on the postmark. I know you don't love me still, I'm not so vain, I just know that you'll be mightily intrigued. And you are one of the few living mortals of whom the word "mightily" indicates a quality. You see, even now, I am never ironic.

Well, I don't want to sound like a French moralist. I am dying without you, and I won't be dying long. But don't come.

Best always,
Frank

Dear: The Pseudo-Message

I am really not particularly interested in your patronizing
my work just because you have never been able to patronize
me personally because you think I'm witty, which I'm not.
What could a square like you possibly find promising in an
ex-chichi poet like myself (as Gregory says in that Dutch
magazine), with all the necessarily elliptical stances of a
brutish soul inhabited by an oversophisticated body whose
only refinement is a taste for great and "trashy" composers.
That's not musical taste, you know.

So it won't seem obscure to you that I don't believe there is
such a thing as metrics. Just the old ear and the young tongue
going into it, and staying; or vice versa, and retrograde, crab-
wise, inverse. I think inverse is ever so much better than
inscape, and I wouldn't shit you. I wouldn't bother.

So goodbye, old pal (my first irony! the irony of which is
not sorrowful masculinity, but the fact that you were never a
pal) and may all the horses greet you (except the one I'm
riding) and may you mend many a stone wall. I suppose you
will think this is an arse pathetica, but that's your problem.

Best always,

O'Hara

Dear: The Note Worth

Now I know probably as much as I will ever know of living.
How perfect and horrible it is! not life, but my self, its magical
composition, which could be taken as an image, but luckily I
don't have to, can not, since I inhabit it. It is that *it* that seems
(that it) so strange.

There is nothing foreign that lives. Everything unknown is
potentially known. Everyone is either brave or gallant, the chief

challenge being to force life to yield its opportunities, personally, to you. What a courageous undertaking, except when, smiling, you pull the pretty ring out of the pineapple and blow yourself up. I guess I'm trying to appeal to you, but you won't be able to cry. If you were here, I would just smile and try not to look wistful, and the effort would allow us both to think of each other.

You seem to know everything I do, and it never embarrasses me. So few people ever wish to know anything! Or you know already.

We never teach each other anything. That is perfect. We've learned a lot about education since the Greeks.

I see you smiling, I see you chewing your lower lip at cocktails. I see you always, your mink, your CHEMISTS FOR CUSTOM—Miss Lang: perfumes, your performance as Miss Northern Lights, tes poèmes, ma carissima, my insincerity, your insincerity, my meanness, your meanness back, yaks, dolors, secrets,

and now you are foreign to me. That is horrible.

My love while I live,
The author

The Stars

They do what we (can) no longer do,
they feel what we no longer (would) feel.
—Po Chü-i

They are greater than we
                    les étoiles soi-disantes et malgré elles
and at last we are liberated
                    from the psychology
                                        of the nonesuch
because they are not they
                    without we-uns telescopy
and what with the leverage of chance and all
they are adorable, discrete, admirable, scandal-free, sweet and
                                                    disruptable
although they are scandalous
                    because the meanness of souls cannot be as waged
although it can be eradicated
                    which no tyrannous power has ever thought of
because tyranny has never known
                            real powers
                                    and anyway
I shall ask you
            I am asking you
                        if you have any idea
                                    and you will mention
AIDA
    and I will say you went home too early for the argument
                                                    but
that will not save you because you use because because you're
                                            drunk
    and I am not so dolce that I can yield my idols to a mess of
                                            shit—

which I eat as I eat the wisdom of Socrates   (if it happens!)
                                        and I think I am good
and I think everybody is good
                        and U wonder why others have difficulties
with
      Allen Ginsberg
                  (I like others' ability with his name because they
at least
            remember it and
                        how many
                              can you say that of) how many can you
disremember
            in daylight
                        and how many more gain their sleep that way
                  Whether 'tis better
                        to be a shit or an archangel $=$ he
                                                is
the same thing without a dick
                        and I despise the coward as is
                                          as is
                                                there
Mayakovsky sails
                  and, ignorant of his sailing,
                                    the false rear their
many-colored sheet; and it is not speed of sex as the guardian
                                                without
                  a hardon said.

                        [September 6–November 1, 1957]

Springtemps

"When it gets into that area
it's like opening a door for
someone"
                Joe comes in with
a new pair of flowers and
we have another May whiskey
                we go
on working, it's more like
the hive that way
            and think
up bee-keeper
                    presents,
                        not
that anything's
    been born yet

it's only the first day, Joe
what did you expect?

To Ned

It's a hot night
and Ned is washing his feet
he never will play that song
Thank god for gin
it makes you hotter and cooler
sweet and sour is better than nothing
and it's nice to be nice
in front of nice people
for a change, a change is nice
but it's not a change

[July 25, 1958]

Platinum, Watching TV, Etc.

Do I feel your hand on my leg? I think I do, and I think
        you want to steal the platinum in my kneecap and
        then fly the country in your little pipe-plane, as you
        sit at your desk pretending to be Virginia Grey

I wish you'd pretend to be Anne Meacham, I adore Anne
        Meacham and besides, she's a genius

that's the way I see it, stubborn as a mule hitched to a
        new EDSEL that won't move because it wasn't built
        to move in the medium (TV never moves, not the
        way words move on the page or paintings move
        inside themselves),

that's why I love Anne so much: she moves inside herself
        and yet the stage is under her, untorn, and underneath
        its somber surface all that platinum is safe, strong,
        glittering in privacy and holding things together

                    [at Norman Bluhm's, March 31, 1958]

189

[There's Nothing More Beautiful]

There's nothing more beautiful
than knowing something is going
to be over
        all day you act like
someone else and then, at dusk,
you go down on someone for the first
time, down, down, as only a boy
like a French horn goes down
on a man. It is the man he will
become, with tears for his lost
will-lessness and the anger of
his former smile
        which was lecherous.
And why not? eager for light,
for liquid, the breath of anticipation,
only acting for himself. When
later he will have begun to die
at the moment he acts for others.

[March 14, 1958]

[Have You Ever Wanted]

Have you ever wanted
to get in the ring
with Tolstoy?

no, but I want
to get into bed
with you

how's that?

Fou-rire

It really is amusing
that for all the centuries of mankind
the problem has been how
to kill enough people
and now
it is how
not to kill them all

[July 28, 1958]

Two Poems and a Half

EUROPE
I think we better start revising our dictionaries.

*

NIGHT
I seem to be following a cat, but when I turn the corner there's
another cat.

*

VENICE
and now I am in Italy.

*

[Summer 1958]

Callas and a Photograph of Gregory Corso

The light fell out of the day
into an energy of the sky
and on the rooftop a sob was gathering
as in the distance a man poled pigeons

like a cloud the little boy
sought the occasion of his falling
and across some river a Greek girl
was screaming at her mother

one day the girl would scream
her hatred at La Scala and he
would suffer love to become bombs

if there were no cameras
I would not know this boy
but hatred becomes beauty anyway
and love must turn to power or it dies

[January 27, 1959]

To Violet Lang

My darling
　　　　it would have been no sacrifice
　　　　　　　　　　to give my life

for yours
　　　　I wish, I am, waiting for you
　　　　　　　　　on the "other side"

offering you a bath
　　　　　　and my new poems to read in it
　　　　　　　　　　everything is gone

except you, really you, you are always with me

　　　　　　　　　　[March 10, 1959]

Poem

I could die
to be here at this time
is too much to bear
but it is fun
as all things are that you reject
as I never wrote down any of the haikus
that I've thought of
because they're not worth writing
and you care so much
or do you?

　　　　　　　　　　[July 26, 1959]

194

University Place

Oh Alice Esty! we are leaving
University Place the day after
your concert and listening to
Rimsky-Korsakov as we think back
on Poulenc's labors and painters.
Our own painters will be heavy in
the morning as the truck pulls up
the hail falls down as it is falling
now. Spain! desire! heliotropes!
where are you? where is Francis P
and dear dead Paul Eluard? where
are we and where tomorrow will we be?

Decay sets in when someone suddenly
stops singing and life becomes a
bad reproduction of Jackson Pollock's
beautiful *Bird Effort* in a magazine
that folded. Where will we go
when we have truly moved, when life
says "Look, you're new, be calm"
and angrily we leave and die.

[March 27, 1959]

[It Is 4:19 in Pennsylvania Station]

It is 4:19 in Pennsylvania Station
and we are running to catch the train for East Hampton
strange train! for it will take us to Patsy and Mike
and how can it? (since we love them and are there)
but we go, because of seeing (how important it is)
and Maxine (why are you here? because of Larry? yes)
and Mary, sweetie, it was lovely having drinks at your studio
and I, for five, enjoyed dinner although nobody else seemed to
because of the portrait of Mamma Lanza
lucas
carey
dottie
joey
daddy
mommy
joey and mike
in a new country where the naps are long
it is in East Hampton where the naps are long
and we have been here before but don't remember which is good

[June 1959]

196

Maria Kurenko (Rachmaninoff Sings)

Oh night, to hear them once again
is if we were at Kyriena's and the moon
over the Hudson were blue no movie
for our lives are movie lives and our
responses movie retaliations for imagined
slights which are only Myrna Loy
worrying about the secretary who wife
never loved her husband while the
secretary probably did but he doesn't
love her. That's what the floods of spring
are like, some stream that never cared about
a bridge comes along and takes it from
the bank that never noticed it anyway.
We are all so very very much mistaken.

[August 12, 1959]

[Why Is David Randolph Such a Jerk]

Why is David Randolph such a jerk
madrigals bull shit if I had any
tangerines left I'd throw them
just like I was shaving the last time
but things aren't as serious now
or else I'm terribly ennuyeux
Bay of Naples Bay of Rum Sausalito
make a madrigal out of that, baby

Kein Traum

Awakening, now, the war has broken out
everything is vicious and cruel
as it really is
we are back in reality
out of cigarettes
dying gorgeously
for an unknown principle
as persons we are abstract
and certain
the smoldering snow is falling
as it did when Liszt died
and the Austro-Hungarian empire
was initiating trouble
a lot of trouble
there was a germ of outrageous desire
it lodged in our hearts
it will never succumb
it is within us
it will never die
but we shall die
and awaken from our torment
in a storm of anguish
which is just
octaves of war
pound through my willing brain
and everything is right again
we are deciduous
like a dead tree
across this vile street
an old lady in a wig is plucking her eyebrows
in the window
death

[September 4, 1959]

[On the Vast Highway]

On the vast highway
where death streams cheerfully
in the sunlight and the enormous spans
cast their 4 o'clock suspensions
over the harbor I am told
of the infidelities of the Puerto Ricans
and the meanness of the Jews
by an Irish cab driver
it is good that there are so many kinds of us
so death can choose
and even perhaps prefer
he who casts the first shadow of the day
on those who are trying to live till dark

[January 1, 1960]

Poem

"We'll probably pay for it in August" the radio says
these beautiful steel days of loneliness, I won't pay

        Grieg's country dances
        Stravinsky's *Norwegian Moods*

I don't think of them as lice, I think of them as crabs
it's my zodiacal sign -0-, all part of the strange slump of summer

                                            [July 8, 1960]

Poem

You do not always seem to be able to decide
that it is all right, that you are doing what you're doing
and yet there is always that complicity in your smile
that it is we, not you, who are doing it
which is one of the things that makes me love you

                                            [July 8, 1960]

Old Copies of *Life* Magazine

Oh god! someone protect the Champs-Élysées
I just saw that Frenchman's face again in tears
they may have reached the Arc de Triomphe
but at least they didn't get it apart
and set it up near the fake Picasso in Hamburg
he was stuck in an ad for a book on World War II

*

In the center of this grey blur
there is quite an ugly costume, but then
how would I know, it may be beautiful
especially in Manchester, in Hants
and along the beautiful brown expanse
of the Gaboon River in a barge
now that we have exchanged all our
cultural traditions so equitably forced

*

Yearly it became grander
bigger thicker familiarer
it began to look fortunate
in the sense of money, smiles
and worked-for disasters

[September 12, 1960]

"Chez William Kramps"

I never seem to hear much, except Tschaikovsky.
What's the matter with me, especially on Saturday
afternoon? it seems that there's a park nearby
and people in it. But luckily they don't drop in
and one can pleasurably collect grievances while being
perfectly confidential and enjoying it a lot. Oh truss!
don't you feel yourself maligned? So do I, darling truss!
but I'm not, really. See that evil glint in my eye?
it's Evil, being friendly for its own sake, and mine.
Well, not being a hip-slinger, I don't need you, truss,
but I love you all the same, that is the same as I love
toothbrushes and jock-straps and inkwells and typography.
What I really love is people, and I don't much care whom
except for a few favorites who fit, which you understand.
It's like the sky being above the earth. It isn't above
the moon, is it? Nor do I like anyone but you and you.

[October 7, 1960]

202

Young Girl in Pusuit of Lorca

Without encountering you
voyager for whom I have prepared this white torso
oh god the air

soon my life will be the moon
I will be far from horses and arguments
and the air will obscure tomorrow

delay the wind
with lightness and licence I will find
the lust of your marshes

you will blame me for grass
you will eat an armload of my anguish
bathe in the dentifrice of my wounds

speak truly of the taste
let the torrent of my cheap temper-ridden heart
become a dove or dope

nudes march by in masks
whole squadrons pretending to be morphodites
doubles of the rocks but full of sweat

come to kiss your hips I heave
I squander my lips on your perfect kneecaps
knowing heaven to be vacant

give me your hand your heart your wrist
your hair and crystal house
your blood-filled stable of rising

you alone question your beauty
prepare to face it in the air of my being
I alone force you to

prepare to face your beauty
but only value our love, our tantrum of belief
more than nothingness

[October 18, 1960]

[How Wonderful It Is That the
  Park Avenue Viaduct Is Being Rehabilitated]

How wonderful it is that the Park Avenue Viaduct is being
                                                rehabilitated
I wish I were too
now the rain is pouring down and it just makes me wet
while the particles of filthy Manhattan air
are filling in the chinks in the viaduct's reconstruction

A Trip to the Zoo

"Just drop over
we'll have dinner and a talk
and afterwards someone'll
come by for drinks
it'll be such fun
to tell you about my little
theory I have
about reading out loud
verse
verse?
it's quite exciting
are there other people really coming?"
and if so when

        *

but it is necessary
to listen
as one is listened to
no it isn't
unless you honestly prefer
Christ to the ostrich

[December 10, 1960]

Dear Vincent,

Affecting
to dissemble
to reassure us
I say I love you
and I do!
I do from a longtime before even
not just now
that it's come up
(or gone down)
but all that time

Frank

[The Fondest Dream of]

The fondest dream of
every American boy
is to go to work and use
his father's typewriter

you spill ink over
his secretary and follow her
to the fainting room
where she fails to wash it off

What Happened to
"The Elephant Is at the Door"

As one who had walked further there was nothing to be seen.
No green basket full of stones, not an iota of de-roach liquid,
not a jam-jar of fresh little palm leaves, nothing. But in the
window four oyster-glass bulbs leaned against the torn dirty
shade. What happened is that the little boy in the hall was
late for school and hurt his ankle and the big fat boy kept
shouting at him to hurry up which made him hurt his ankle.
In the first place the fat boy was a little prick. And the school
is big and dirty and so on.

Later on there were no eggs and no cheese crunchies. No
nothing. The sky was blue and the street was wet. The wind
blew through the park through all the old Lithuanians. I had
a friend who liked living in a Lithuanian neighborhood be-
cause he was Lithuanian but couldn't speak Lithuanian, he
just was it. He was very handsome so it didn't much matter
where he lived.

Then there is another friend of mine who was just dogged
by good fortune and there is another friend whose dogs got
away and wounded another dog belonging to an old man of
that neighborhood. I have another friend who likes to live in
Paris because he is from St. Malo and another friend who likes
to live there because of the other friend and various other
reasons not having anything to do with being French. That's
the American way, that's not Slav at all. I once knew a Pan-
Slavist who wanted to live in Panama but never could some-
how. He lives in Brooklyn Heights. She, rather. She actually
only wanted to live in Panama after reading Jane Bowles'
Two Serious Ladies, part of which takes place there I believe.

[February 10, 1961]

After a Meeting of *The 2nd Coming*

Well that's one war you didn't win Bill
even if you are as valiant as Lumumba
it's hard to reach people if they don't read
and you can't very well send in a UN
Task Force—they're all subscribers to that
as a matter of fact they seem to think they're it

but don't be discouraged there are still
some corpses in the old corral at least there
were the last time I looked and how
could they move yes I know there's that big
well-organized group of corpse-pushers
there should be a law! rolling those corpses
from quarterly to quarterly like a girl with a
hoop
        it's just like this here honoring the
arts on political occasions who could like it
except if'n you been lugging those rocks (not
necessarily in jail) and you got this burning
to be part of your bloody society like a spinster
or something and finally you get to travel
and what happens you can't even see anything
that's politics for you
                        but as I was inferring
I think that it's wonderful to have gone to
a meeting and come out alone it's what in France
they call singular, unless you're De Gaulle
then they call it giraffe well it is giraffe
and I think we united states should stick
together because it's all they have

[February 21, 1961]

Poem During Poulenc's *Gloria*

The sweet sounds of the Seine
drift slowly along inside my left shoulder blade
it is slightly like a stiff neck
                                only in the back
how strange! we don't know each other
                                what faintly purposeful motives lead
us to such odd ends
                        and that they are ends   stops
what stops
                nothing but a moment of thoughtful tranquillity
unless it's pleasant you hasten
                                I hasten

                                no
I did not say hello to you when you wanted me to deliberately
and you deliberately wanted me
                                not to
                                so you
could gracefully complain
                                which is again almost
the only graceful thing anyone could do
as you so well know
                        just as hurt is the only beautiful
now that we are grown up
                                but I don't find the rewards
actual as you do
                        only in thinking about it
I would rather know someone happy and vulgar
but who could love
                        Manon more than Marlene Dietrich
for that matter, (first comma)
                                who could love me

more than you

        though you are a mean almost (another almost)
vicious person

        and I am really beautiful beside you
if anyone knew you but me

        you wouldn't be beautiful
if you hadn't read Proust

        but I would

        this poem
is called "a tantrum" by "the bappy few" or will be

        unless of course they are too few to know
this all seems spiritual to me

        it must be against god, too (second comma)

        [July 6, 1961]

The Trout Quintet

Okay let's go swimming
I don't want to
well then don't
I want some peanut butter
I want some cream soda

last night the moon seemed to say something
it said "eat"
I said there's nothing
it mentioned plankton
but it had all drifted away

do you think the sand
kills stones

(keep rippling)
no I don't think that
I'm still rippling

well who ever said anything's
done at Radio City Music Hall
except the bolero
but who's ever seen it
who asked

you will think the light
comes from somewhere else
but it comes from the floor
otherwise you wouldn't see it
you're always looking down

after the swim I sat
and rubbed the sand into my crotch
I want to go
to Spain
where the olive trees

[July 6, 1961]

F.Y.I. #371 (The Nun)

I just saw a nun in blue walking along with a valise
in one hand and a package in the other wrapped
with brown paper and tied with white string
it was astounding
she was completely defenseless she couldn't even have
scratched herself if bitten by a bug
unless of course she dropped the package or the valise
after which epiphany the heavenly glass doors opened
(I opened them)
and I was back at work
now I will have to wait till four o'clock for something
interesting to happen
this isn't Manhattan this is hell

F.Y.I. # 371a (Haiku Day For The Nuns)

stripping   elbow at 10
scratch   tie
another Yipe!   blue
Primo Carnera   kitty
              kat
     *   tendon
              brown
              blood
Yet the act   10
        u
         a   *   *

far less of it is known than (glassy) thunk

l feeling of it all was sort of like wind blowing up the fringes to reveal two huge watermelons squashing a rose, right there in front of the Donnel Public Free Reading & Record Library facade, not hurruffying, but not very
illuminating, either. (That's where the "glassy" came in—see 3rd haiku.)
        *

F.Y.I. #371b (Parallel Forces, Excerpted)

Stripping the nun tied up her kittykat with blue string her elbow

                                                   bled

and a carnation fell defenselessly to the glass floor

                                      (onto a bug!)

       far less of a scratch than a package

   the watermelon wrapped in paper got bitten into it's all brown

a muscular reading of what four o'clock would bring

                                     interesting

     that in Manhattan thunk is pronounced library

     hell is your epiphany being no nun

                                    [July 10, 1961]

Le Domaine Muscial

"Like a barbershop that's closed on Saturdays"

Prepare to assuage the rock in the room!
overlooking the sea!
drip and tear at the pain in those cement vials!
accept responsibility for clouds walking the earth!
drape yourself over the curtain rod and fall to the floor!
halt the white horse on its way to the statue of George

                                  Washington!

pick up after him! like Chariot!
make me an offer!
kiss me like glue!
wait endlessly in the street outside a black window!
the streetlamp is flickering out!

a letter floats down!
the letter floats down the gutter into the sewer! the hydrant's
                                        turned on!

beaten on the back beaten on the back! by . . . !
your wrists ache from reaching for the letter!
your shoes are wet!
fungus!
your feet splay like hands the bloody cracks!
try to wrench the phone away from your breasts! akh!
a serpent is crawling out of your navel!
it has the face of your lover!
it is kissing you softly deftly as a fly walks!
you are tossing and turning in a strange sheet!
it's the wrong color for a shroud!
you are disgraced humiliated and wronged through the window!
you are indecent bestial calm!
you are distorted!
eat eat keep up your strength it's going to get worse!
drink drink yourself into a stupor because you are stupid!
give up reasons!
something is stirring down there!
the stranger is rising!
walk to work!
drown in the yoghurt flowing over the front of the apartment
                                        house!

flames!
ashes!
lava!
pot!
                    the stars are out

                                [July 28, 1961]

[Like a Barbershop That's
   Closed on Saturday, Me Heart]

Like a barbershop that's closed on Saturday, me heart
can hardly bear to send off our St. Bridget poems to
Barney Rosset, it's our CHEE-EYE-ULD! never left your
house or my house before! so I buy a small container of
pepper and throw it in me eyes so I won't see the stamps.
"But if everybody did what they wished, everybody
would be doing what they wanted."WNYC (City Councilman,
German-Jewish extraction.)

Off the Kerb
& After Emily Dickinson
(Sonnet)

Walking home through the mist tonight
I almost stepped on two mice
I hated them
not because they were mice
but because I almost stepped on them
funny,
I am always almost being stepped on too
I suppose those giants feel the same about me
on their way

[August 23, 1961]

Shooting the Shit Again

I was rattling along thinking—what was I thinking of?
I guess it was of the Coastguard Beach (or was it *trois corbeaux*?)
dans le spleen de la jeunesse dorée, je suis las de vivre au pays
                                      fatal
I was also thinking how much I like the flan de la jeunesse dorée
I think Martha Foley is a very nice woman, too, so are you
just because I love you doesn't make me a woman unless it
                              makes you one too (so
fuck you, you can't put me in a "false" position—anyway all you
                                 ever talk about
is Robert Lowell any more) nyaaaaa! piss on your adaluvian head
I think you have a suspicion I'd like that, damn that private eye for
                                  squealing
oh god it's hard for anything to get dirty enough any more . . .
oh god it's hard . . .
and if you think that's the typewriter you're nuts . . .

                                [September 4, 1961]

[How Poecile and Endearing Is the Porch]

How poecile and endearing is the Porch
it lingers there in the dying light
school of fish, scared and wise
Sappho is teaching Socrates is
teaching Virgil is teaching Nadia
and Ned everyone is teaching someone
this is Greek civilization! Come on in

                                [December 7, 1961]

Conglomerations in the
Snow of Christmas Eve 1961

After the violent depressions of two weeks
you see clear
                        into the snow like hail of afternoon,
going to a wedding party One Fifth Avenue

at the top of my heart is happiness and love
Howie and Mary Vincent Joe Arnold Norman
missing Carey missing Jane Nettie and LeRoi,
at the bottom:
                        "Who is this guy?
                        Eddie Bartlett
                        How are you hooked up with him?
                        I never figured it out
                        What was his business?
                        He used to be a big shot"
                in the snow, the never-ending snow of luck
                and Russian recordings
I hate all that I hate almost everything I am the very figger
                        of Christmas present

I do love wedding celebrations though, they
                        get somewhere

and besides it's so horrible not to be able to remember
the finger variation and the hand variation from *Sleeping Beauty*
that is, which is which when encountered on the radio

Un Homme Respectueux

to, for and about Virgil Thomson

The ends are not tied up
                              everything is open fields
and the wheat looks like staves in Rossini
            the snow falls and falls
                              but in sunlight
gloom?
            it's an anemone, he dropped it in the snow

you fix the stove, you get the screwdriver and it all
bangs and crashes and you sweat
                              it's for cooking, the fixing
Bohemians get out of taxicabs, rose-colored as gigot

[1961]

Le Boeuf sur le Toit

to V. R. Lang

And I do nothing new
because I love you now,
this is an epithalamium
I guess. Where did all
the Dubonnet go and the
trips to Revere? We
crowned the Minuteman at
Concord with weeds one
dawn and now you're gone.

The years are heavier for
being faster, they grind, they
grind—it was fun while it
lasted and frightful that
it lasts. Do you know what
really light music is? it
expires on the spit. And you say
"Who is Jane?" I say "It's true,
dear, New York has brutalized Frank!"

My Day

There I was sitting at work
                    reading *Stephen Hero*
when suddenly the snow
                    started falling falling softly, etc.
and I was waiting for Carey to show up
          to go see *Swingtime*
                            in the
auditorium under farunder the museum where
I often like to go
                  January is the cruellest
being neither February nor December
                      and so
we went down down into the bowels of the modernest
art
    accepting no Millard Fabric so testy were we
where is that elevator

                              [January 24, 1962]

[I Will Always Remember]

I will always remember
that I have put that comma
in, so you would not
be connected with anyone
but me, in the air at sea

       where a strange figure
       smoke a cigarette the bent air
       an establishment of niceties
       you have concocted me

     when the dithyramb accepts
     itself as Henri-Matisse, fortune
     smiles the glass "darkens" ouch

there can be no distinguishable
an open manhole welcomes the taxi
ouch
I wanted to lounge in the lounge
the wave swept over me

       so I cannot be connected
       with anyone but you

                  [March 22, 1962]

Poem

Hoopla! yah yah yah
in the concentration camp   white hope
we always flicked it off that way   hot lead
to show the melody of Informers   a banana bandana and your
and then the spangled eyelids   what the heap said to the eagle
closed their mouths for   and then the news
a moment of thought-out noise   I want nothing of
"a gossipy novel can sink a ship"
the billboard said   "Charlie Brown you are a traitor
and all the heads agreed sagely
It's better to be known only   eclipsed ugliness
to your (soi disant) lover   he's nice to have around
                                  disappear
      what we will often wonder about, and long

Poem

It's faster if you late but may never occur the pleasant surprise of narr
a constitutional   a vest of changing mores   well the nuts
    you roomed over the garage that decade on a tutorship   well
the ambiguities were flowering over the cesspool and the spit dried
        it was a fantastic sortie into the disagreeable
absolutes, everywhere absolutes!
my life is changing!

                          [July 7, 1962]

To Lotte Lenya

Heute morgen, I was moreorless "up"

                                    waiting for everybody
but everybody never comes you're lucky if anybody does
in an empty house buried in grass near the sea
das Meer das Lied die Liebe, err, der Lieb', alles ist aufgesetzt
      but the whirlwind in the tabletop
      an anguished cry from the toilet
      a corrective paw in the sink
      your lilacs brown as a berry spinning

I was not really waiting

Lawrence

So that you might see
the odd nature of an
just catastrophe you
might know the periphery
you might sense the
noeud; and then it would
be very boring. But as
it is it will be interest-
ing and fairly moving
when everything goes down
and the end seems like
sunset "in" the "river."
The postcard has been "sent."
I will say "march!" and it
will not be interesting, and
you will say "February,"
and I will not be interested.
It will be gone away, and
neither of us will have moved.
Sic transit Mesopotamia.
He is not ill, he is just
determined, as the weak-willed
will follow dreams, instead
of hallucinations, there.
This is not an opinion.
There is a lot of sand in it.
It's the general health.

[July 28, 1962]

Song

I ate out your heart
while I was drifting through the rain
a strange autumnal smoke
drifted up my cigarette and it tasted
of steeple and mud
where I had advanced to a sign read god
bless our little field
but it meant nothing to me so far beyond
what created this heavy shrine
left sitting beside the railroad for
memorial purposes
memory of fun of hopes of sickness and doubt

[September 5, 1962]

Pedantry

the strange fragrance of skyscrapers
what has it to do with Lakmé or slums
the hot sun the middling dessert
the casual pain of anxious thought
"because of you" "I thought that you"
jungle traffic   an herbarium
the center of selfish concerns
composed in 1776   at Yaddo
you will not eat this dinner again
wuth your tusk   but the moon
still floats over the shit-filled canal
and will continue to float until
the pills arrive   and the dreary earth
the bells ring and the orange-soaked temple
expires with a sigh of boredom

[September 6, 1962]

Poem

in that red
there was very little difference
in what was good
and what would happen

227

[What Strange Cataract the Peculiar]

what strange cataract the peculiar
perfume seeping into
                    the haze of feeling
a dynamic loss like the gentian
an a
        a, a, a, the blue steel mill the
effort and a fight afterwards in the street
towards which the cranes are flying
and the pillow is plowing and the orgasm
is nearing it is all happening in the
street where it should in the cold light
of many disinterested eyes you told
them to be there and they are there and
we are not there too as in a battle

[October 21, 1962]

[The Ancient Ache, Quick False Move]

The ancient ache, quick false move
    fires smoldering today on the plaine des Jarres
an apparent failure of the rain forest
    you have thrust your saber into your left foot

meanwhile President Gronchi addressed
    the Supreme Schools when they closed
he tried to make a no-nonsense arrangement
    the sun disappeared on the beach, swam

April came and went the advisers
    were killing more and more persuaded natives
and the buildings were loaned to the
    survivors as they went up in flames for

their principles! their religious
    principles if you can believe in sitting
immolation! an alienated landscape dotted
    with crisp human torches and smudge-pots

your lace sent across the sea and drowned
    in salt the piteousness of wracks, pins
all stretching and drying devices for the spiders
    crumpling fistlike in the revolution

Poem

(after a poem by Ruth Krauss)

lost lost
where are you
lost in the shine
of my nails in the
little blue vein
inside my wrist lost
you are shining the
skin in the sun on
the front of my shoes
in my hair which is
shining with you lost
lost

lost
where are you lost
in my eyes are you
lost in the shine of my
nails in the little
blue vein inside my wrist
lost you are shining
the skin in the sun
on the front of my
shoes in my hair which
is shining with you lost
lost

lost
I want you lost
backyard lost alley the
mountain top and the
looking-glass water
lost lost I want you
lost lost stones lost
shells and the roar that is
lost and the looking-glass
water

[I Know That You Try
  Even Harder Than I]

I know that you try even harder than I
to hold off the darkness and it seems
that the poets that embrace it don't even
feel it at all, it's like taking a shower
to them or their therapy-tears or the
vitally informative sensitivity pill
that makes even Aldous Huxley see color.

[Not to Confirm Dolors with a Wild Laugh]

Not to confirm dolors with a wild laugh
                              or a Federal Reserve Bank stare
whose esthetic ambition is
                    to see it ugly and see it whole,
the misery-lovers,
                  the shame-makers, all trying to be their version
of honest,
          in love with the verb "to be," inaction in action, how rare
is a real
            stance in full bloom! with a drop of rain on it, not wet
Did you ever try
                to kick a sparrow in the shin,
                                        to strangle a hog,
to drown yourself?
                emphatic physical ambitions are just as dubious . . .

[Long as the Street Becomes]

Long as the street becomes
she told me I'd be safe here
a Negro man with a yellow cane
goes into the church comes
right back out hat swinging

keep Tommy away from here go
to your sister's did you hear
do you understand how it feels
to know you're going to get
away you're going to get out

the grass is getting green
nobody stays up to water it
like in Madrid where everyone
stays up to water the simple
grass and us simple too

praying antennae outstretched
for news of the news of the world
there's a lot of traffic for a
quiet country road you stifle me
why do you keep me from having men

friends of my own race

[1964]

[Just as I am Not Sure Where Everything Is Going]

Just as I am not sure where everything is going
I am not sure that everything is going
To be a kiss for the bump of literature or a hug
For the heartline's fizzle though I know what I like
And it doesn't have to have soda added (to it)
For instance, if Tolstoy was a Pharisee, what does that make
You or me. Art isn't musack for the moujiks after all.
Mop please, would you please buy me a mop.
After all I am Fräulein aus der Ohe and it is 1891
and the pain! with me playing my head off and
Tschaikovsky sobbing in B flat in Carnegie Hall
while it's trying to open and he's trying to conduct!
He saw clearly the limitations as well as the technical
value of the art of Gertrude Stein and James Joyce. (Of.)
Ebbing! Ebbing! Ebbinge-Wubben and the Oderfluss.
I sat watching an Alp and rails from the Ruhr
turned into milch cows in my agonized gauze,
and now you can see what kind of men you all have raised.

Raysse Beach, Water Island, Louse Point, Newport Beach, tell me,
What negroes have lain down deep in your black under-sand ?
Stands lubricrushkandoolamperanthusian-sloop—all negroes,
All white fools for the negro
                                        an iffen yo cain't ketch 'em
              understand, Willy ? that's a bison, yeah, a rectangle, yeah—
hecata hecata hecata
                          read the weak, walked-out-asséd bouk
                                        sens de la vie
              and you can't get around it
                                        hecata hecata hecata
algae of the water-soul, food for thought

[April 18, 1965]

[Why Are There Flies
   on the Floor]

Why are there flies on the floor
in February, and the snow mushing outside
and the cats asleep?
                    Because you came
back from Paris, to celebrate your return.

[February 2, 1966]

NOTES ON THE POEMS

NOIR CACADOU, OR THE FATAL MUSIC OF WAR; A BYZANTINE
PLACE; A CALLIGRAM; LINES ACROSS THE UNITED STATES; POEM (I
Can't wait for spring!); POEM (Poised and cheerful the); POEM (Suppose that
grey tree, so nude); POEM (Green things are flowers too); SONG (I'm going
New York!)
These poems were included in "A Byzantine Place," O'Hara's Hopwood thesis.

A DOPPELGÄNGER
On MS x278 O'Hara wrote "John Ashbery" by the first stanza, "Lyon Phelps" by
the second, "George Montgomery" by the third, and "Ed Hale" by the fourth.

A PATHETIC NOTE
MS 355 has the earlier title "A Pathetic Note to George Montgomery" with the
second phrase inked out.

A BYZANTINE PLACE
MS 132 has the original dedication "to George Montgomery" canceled.

POEM (Just as I leave the theatre)
MS 586 has these three canceled alternative last lines:
> We would have interested Donne!
> Everything eventually happens!
> Hello to the whole world!
and below the poem: (Brodkey)

AN EPILOGUE: TO THE PLAYERS OF *TRY! TRY!*
The first version of *Try! Try!* was produced by the Poets' Theatre on February
26, 1951, with Violet Lang, John Ashbery and Jack Rogers playing the three
roles. O'Hara was unable to attend.

VOYAGE À PARIS
MS 698 indicates this poem was written during a G. B. Harrison lecture at Ann
Arbor, March 1951.

A PORTRAIT
MS 116 has the earlier title "A Portrait of Rimbaud" with the last two words
crossed out, and a canceled last line to the first section:
> Tohu-bohu and plain boohoo:

THE SOLDIER
MS 140 has this deleted final stanza:

> Don't doubt the sea can drive you mad
> for I've loved vessels you could not
> believe desire would welcome and I tell
> you death is only ordinary things alone

FORM AND UTTERANCE
MS 573 has "Duchamp" written below the poem.

SKY RHYMES
MS 593 is signed: Charles Brockden Brown

A VIRTUOSO
MS 192 has these last lines:

> madly up hill! "Oh to be at Winterthur
> now that Schoenberg's dead, he's gone
> to join John Keats, he has!" And while
> millions of roses fall from our pianist's
> cuffs no one thinks of anything but
> those marvellous fists knocking out
> those beautiful presensible teeth.

A CLASSICAL LAST ACT
SERENADE (Starlings are singing)
A ROMANTIC POET TO HIS MUSE
These poems are signed "Arnold Cage," perhaps derived from Arnold Schoenberg and John Cage.

SCHOENBERG
The phrase "false Florimells" perhaps derives from Spenser's *The Faerie Queene*.

GRACE AND GEORGE, AN ECLOGUE
Grace Hartigan's nom de brosse in the early fifties was "George Hartigan." (Credit: Bill Berkson.)

JACOB WRESTLING
In MS 400 lines 3–5 originally read:

> shoulder don't argue out
> the struggle in the dentist's
> chair. Should I frame

THE BEACH IN APRIL
In MS x294 "changing roadsters" in line 16 was originally "chancey busters," and "practicing" in line 20 was "playing."

[TENT-DIGGING ON THE VACANT LAKES WE APPLED]
MS 605 has these additional canceled last lines:
> The janitor is browning a witch behind the orchard.
> If all their fears were imprisoned I'd float
> onto the meadowy regrets of a bronze plaque,
> an air which reduces the mannerism to a menace.

POEM (The rich cubicle's enclosure)
MS x541 has "Wyndham Lewis or Vortex" written below the poem.

A WREATH FOR JOHN WHEELWRIGHT
MS 404 adds this last line to stanza 2:
> running for Congress knew your first name.

and gives 8 deleted lines from the beginning of stanza 3:
> Ah. "The most random gifts are most comfortable.
> We must do what we can where we are. Lord Jesus
> did not move to Chicago, son, nor Churchill open
> a bazaar. When the day comes for you to prove
> your love, my own little boy, you'll have Jehovah
> on your right hand and MacPherson on your left.
> Don't waste a move. Play close to your chest. You
> are in the great tradition of airplane engineers."

In the last line of stanza 4 "Jordan!" and "He" have been crossed out and "God?" and "it" substituted.

CLOUDS
In MS x595 the last two lines are marked: Omit?
MS x513 dates it: 1954.

ST. SIMEON
MS x707 has a deleted earlier title: Faun

ADDICT-LOVE
Earlier titles were: Homage to Michaux. They Auction off Goldberg's Possessions. MS 543 has this epigraph:
> "Ah, my dear, how palpable is the approach of spring!
> My heart beats as though it were expecting someone."
> > —Gogol

FOREST DIVERS
BRIDLEPATH
These poems are from Ben Weber's MSS.

TSCHAIKOVSKIANA
PALISADES
BILL'S BODY SHOP
A LITTLE ON HIS RECENTNESS
[THERE'S SUCH AN I LOVE YOU!]
DEAR BOBBY
These poems are from Robert Fizdale's MSS.

SONNET (O at last the towers)
MS 394 has "power" substituted for the canceled "a man" in line 3.

AUGUSTUS
Merle Marsicano called this poem "Jet Pears" for a dance in her April 3, 1954
concert at Henry Street Playhouse. She writes: "Yes. I spoke it backstage through
a sound system . . . I had Frank to a rehearsal in order that he should be satisfied
as to how I was reading his poem and he seemed well pleased. The whole piece
—dance with reading—was highly successful." MM to DA April 1, 1976.

POEM (Here we are again together)
From Ben Weber's MS. Weber's settting of the first stanza, for soprano and
piano, was published as Song Opus 44 in *Folder* 4,1956; his setting of the second
stanza has not been published.

[IN THE PEARLY GREEN LIGHT]
MS 630 has two canceled last lines:
    "the incense is for you" I babble,
    but I know I'm still in bed.

MOVIE CANTATA
In MS x611 an earlier title "A History of the Movies" has been crossed out and
"Fragment" substituted; the divisions are called cantos. A later reworking for a
cantata (MS x299) is given here.

EPIGRAM FOR JOE
MS 303 has a canceled earlier title: "Light"; and two canceled last lines:
    "I've been swimming for hours, it's freezing!"
    I smile as the enormous waves take me aboard.

[NOW IT SEEMS FAR AWAY AND GENTLE]

In January 1957 O'Hara sent the following note to Philip Guston with this earlier version of his poem "It Seems Far Away and Gentle Now," which has "(Guston, Painting, 1954)" typed at bottom of the MS:

> Dear Philip,
>
> This little meditation I'm enclosing probably is too personal to have much directly to do with it, but it was inspired by your Painting in the Museum [of Modern Art's] collection (most recently it was hanging on the 3rd floor landing during the British show) so I thought I'd send it to you. . . .
>
> Sincerely,
Frank

CORRESPONDING FOREIGNLY

This poem is titled "Niagara Fails" in MS x574.

BAGATELLE, OR THE IMPORTANCE OF BEING LARRY AND FRANK

This poem is from Larry Rivers' MS.

COLLECTED PROSES, AN ANSWER

First published in *semi-colon* 11:1 1955, as "An Answer" to Kenneth Koch's "Collected Poems" published in the same issue, and collected in *Thank You and Other Poems* (1962).

CHOPINIANA

From the *Poetry* Magazine Archives, University of Chicago Library.

[IT IS 1:55 IN CAMBRIDGE. PALE AND SPRING COOL,]
TO JOHN ASHBERY ON SZYMANOWSKI'S BIRTHDAY

These poems are from Larry Rivers' MSS.

EPISODE

MS x359 consists of two pages folioed 5 and 6; pages 1–4 seem not to have survived.

Gregory Corso in "The Literary Revolution in America" (Litterair Passpoort, November 1957) wrote: "In New York the more recent poets, especially three ex-chichi academics, Kenneth Koch, Frank O'Hara, John Ashbery, are shifting to freer sympathies, lines, and language."

THE STARS

First published in *Big Sky* 8, 1974.

SPRINGTEMPS
From *Stones* (1958).

TO NED
From Ned Rorem's autograph book.

[THERE'S NOTHING MORE BEAUTIFUL]
MS x561 has these last lines marked "omit":

A

    moment in the history of greatness
    solely and singularly insignificant;
    to oblige is to descant the soul.

TO VIOLET LANG
First published in V. R. Lang: *Poems & Plays* (1975)

KEIN TRAUM
MS x312 gives the title as: Keiner Traum.

POEM (You do not always seem to be able to decide)
In MS 476 the last line is crossed out and queried.

YOUNG GIRL IN PURSUIT OF LORCA
MS x466 has a canceled earlier title: After Lorca. The musical setting by Peter
Hartman in the MS Department, Lilly Library, Indiana University, omits the
last line.

WHAT HAPPENED TO "THE ELEPHANT IS AT THE DOOR"
"The Elephant Is at the Door" was to have been the name of a literary magazine
Diane di Prima and A. B. Spellman projected in 1960. Cf. *The Floating Bear*, vii
(1973).

AFTER A MEETING OF *THE 2ND COMING*
The Second Coming was a short-lived magazine of the period.

THE TROUT QUINTET
In MS x410 the first stanza has these two canceled last lines:
    I think you're awful
    I am

[HOW POECILE AND ENDEARING IS THE PORCH]
From Edwin Denby's MS. Published in *The Poetry Project Newsletter* 17, July 1,
1974.

CONGLOMERATIONS IN THE SNOW OF CHRISTMAS EVE 1961
MS x563 has this canceled last line:
> where is Goddard Lieberson?

and the following written below the poem:
> I think perfection and love have nothing
> to do with each other at all. BW

POEM (Hoopla! yah yah yah)
LAWRENCE
First published in *Big Sky* 8,1974.

[WHAT STRANGE CATARACT THE PECULIAR]
MS x443 has this canceled last stanza:
> you can't tell me this is not vrai
> because it's not charmant I am looking
> at you and at the iridescent truce

POEM (lost lost)
First published in *The World* 7, October 1967.

[I KNOW THAT YOU TRY EVEN HARDER THAN I]
[NOT TO CONFIRM DOLORS WITH A WILD LAUGH]
These were first published in *Fathar* 1, 1970.

INDEX OF TITLES AND FIRST LINES

Titles of poems are given in italic type